Is God
the Only Reliable
Father?

Diane Tennis

The Westminster Press
Philadelphia

Unless otherwise identified, Scripture quotations are from the Revised Standard Version of the Bible, copyrighted 1946, 1952, © 1971, 1973 by the Division of Christian Education of the National Council of the Churches of Christ in the U.S.A., and are used by permission.

Scripture quotations marked TEV are from *Good News Bible: The Bible in Today's English Version*. Old Testament: © American Bible Society, 1976; New Testament: © American Bible Society, 1966, 1971, 1976.

Book design by Gene Harris

First edition

Published by The Westminster Press®
Philadelphia, Pennsylvania

PRINTED IN THE UNITED STATES OF AMERICA
2   4   6   8   9   7   5   3   1

Library of Congress Cataloging in Publication Data

Tennis, Diane.
　　Is God the only reliable father?

　　Bibliography: p.
　　1. God—Fatherhood. 2. Fatherhood (Theology) 3. Sex role—Religious aspects—Christianity. 4. Jesus Christ—Person and offices. I. Title.
BT153.F3T46 1985　　231'.1　　84-20899
ISBN 0-664-24594-3 (pbk.)

Is God the Only Reliable Father?

To Mark and Scott
and to all the children

Contents

1

God as Reliable Father

Do not abandon God the Father. There is danger in abandoning the Father image. To abandon the Father is to abandon the hope of embracing half the race. It is, by default, to stamp approval on the existing sinful alienation of the sexes. It is a status quo strategy, a way of saying, I give up; there is no way for the sexes to live together; we may just as well go our own way.

Do not abandon God the Father, because God as Father is a reliable male symbol in the lives of women and men. Holding on to that reliable Father God can be a way of informing and challenging the status quo. For human fathers are experienced as unreliable. Divorce and custody statistics and a preoccupation with work are the most obvious illustrations of fathers' abandonment of children. By contrast, God as Father does not abandon. If God the Father is reliable, surely he expects reliability from earthly fathers. And so can we! A reliable Father God is a source of calling men into fathering. A reliable Father God is a source of judgment on unreliable sexual arrangements, a source of hope for women and for the fatherless, a symbol emerging out of our loss, luring itself into existence.

God's Reliability

One of the characteristics of the biblical God, is, in fact, reliability. Reliability is precisely how Yahweh was experi-

enced by Israel. Yahweh initiated covenants with Israel.
Covenants were agreements between two parties. Covenants were bound by oaths and carried obligations. That
Yahweh initiated covenants with Israel illustrates, among
other things, Yahweh's eagerness for the relationship.
That Yahweh repeated saving covenants illustrates, among
other things, Yahweh's tenacity in that relationship.

God covenants with Noah to save him and his family to
participate in a re-creation after the world perishes. God
covenants with Abraham and Sarah for their descendants
to inherit the land. God covenants the presence of the
spirit in the prophets and in the Gospels. Jeremiah, for
example, promises a new covenant written on the hearts of
people (Jer. 31:31–33). Joel anticipates the time when
Yahweh will pour out the spirit on all humankind (Joel
2:28). Jesus reveals to the woman at the well that God is
spirit. True worshipers worship in spirit (John 4:23–24).
Jesus promises the gift of the spirit (John 15:26—16:7).
The foundation and model for Yahweh's covenant making
is with Moses on Sinai: "Keep my covenant, [and] you shall
be my own possession among all peoples" (Ex. 19:5). That
covenant is renewed in different forms, in different situations, and with different people, but the story line is the
same. The dominant covenant throughout is this: "I will be
your God, and you shall be my people" (Jer. 7:23).

Israel's obligation in that arrangement, of course, was to
keep the commandments. There were often disastrous
consequences for Israel's failure to do so. Floods and
famine nearly destroyed Israel. Its history is full of want
and warfare. God was reliable, all right. God could be
counted on to withhold and punish with a severity that
would bring a blush to the most hardened human patriarch.

Because of that patriarchal symbol of dominance and
violence and its concomitant suffering, many feminists are
reluctant to use the father symbol as a resource for
reliability or for anything else. This reluctance is often

based on a flaw in thinking, however. The flaw is to use "Father" almost interchangeably with masculine titles and patriarchal symbols. Even in our culture we have some experience or image of a man who is the patriarch in "his" family. He is the master, in charge without checks or balances. If he chooses to be a tyrant, he is a tyrant. Sometimes this tyrant is confused with the word "father." Sometimes all Yahweh's names are confused with Yahweh as "Father." Sometimes *any* behavior of Yahweh's is attributed to his fathering. So, for example, the wrath of Yahweh becomes an activity of Yahweh's fathering. In this scenario, God as Father is indeed terrible.

Let us not confuse the *parent* images of God with *other* images that are more likely to represent domination and violence. In chapter 4 we will examine some of the distinguishing characteristics of parenting symbols in the Bible. Those parenting symbols cannot be identified with any or all of the vast dimensions of Yahweh's character willy-nilly.

Even when God is not specifically named as parent, however, that God did *not* do two very significant things that distinguish Yahweh from some human father images: He did not abandon the children, and he did not destroy them. God was, instead, present and available. He led and loved. He also punished, but he did not leave them.

Nor did he utterly destroy them. There was always a remnant of Israelites who survived God's judgment. The remnant is the smaller number of people who are left after disasters. It is they who are faithful. It is they who bear and represent the continuing existence of the covenant community. The covenant with Noah is a renewed covenant with a remnant. Noah and his family are the remnant, as the only survivors of the flood. They bridge the old and the new through the *unbroken* covenant relationship with Yahweh. In this case the remnant is one family. Even as the prophets railed against the practices of their people, they held out the hope of life for and through a remnant. Sometimes the remnant is from all of Israel (Isa. 46:3).

Sometimes the remnant is from the northern kingdom
(Jer. 31:8), sometimes the south (Isa. 37:31). Sometimes
the remnant is from Jerusalem (Neh. 1:2). Sometimes the
remnant is a large number of people, such as the tribe of
Judah (Hos. 1:7; Mic. 2:12). Always the remnant is whoever within tribe or nation keeps the covenant with
Yahweh. Sometimes there is the expectation that one
person is the remnant in a special way and rules over the
remnant in a special way. Micah (5:1–2) expects that special
remnant ruler to be born in Bethlehem. For the church,
Jesus is the individual remnant *par excellence*. The remnant
represented, among other things, a *permanent existence* of
the two parties to the covenant.

Who then were the children of God? They were the
children of Israel, the children of faith. As the children of
the faithful, they were the children of the surviving remnant. The apostle Paul uses the language of children of
God to mean believers, the inheritors of the new covenant.
There is one image of special children and a special
remnant that is additional good news. The poor are the
remnant (Jer. 39:10; Zeph. 3:12). Micah is one of the
prophets who announces that God will gather the remnant
from among the suffering and the lame (Mic. 4:6–7).
Yahweh moves to save the children of the needy (Ps. 72).
There is special love and care for the orphan child (Mal.
3:5; Isa. 1:17). The oppressed always have a special place
in Yahweh's life. Indeed, the foundational model of covenant and remnant is the saga of Yahweh's delivery of the
children of Israel out of slavery. Even when they preferred
slavery, such a thing was intolerable to Yahweh, who
insisted that they be free. Nearly always it was a collective
Israel that constituted the children of God as one body and
one heir of the covenant. An individual was not considered
a child of God. Indeed, the accusation that Jesus was a
blasphemer proves how dangerous it was to claim individual kinship. When we think of Israel collectively as the
one heir of God's promises, it is even more attractive and

persuasive to image a father metaphor as the one who creates, not destroys. God as Father does not abandon and does not destroy.

God's patriarchal behavior is also present, to be sure. Nevertheless, Yahweh is reliable. He keeps his promises. The covenant maker keeps his part of the deal and follows through. Furthermore, as a father symbol, Yahweh can be counted on to accept the core responsibilities of parenting. Whether or not we agree with some of his other characteristics, he is a reliable father image. He does not reject the children through abandonment or death. Instead, he is present to them and with them. He is a Father who really fathers. That image of a Father God is a judgment on earthly fathers who abandon or destroy. He is also a judgment on broken promises, especially those promises broken to the children. Finally, that Father God calls men into fathering. That God insists on the responsibilities of parenting, especially the core responsibility of maintaining the relationship. For better or worse, the Steadfast One is *always* their father.

An Exclusively Male God as Father

Much current feminist literature catalogs the reasons for *male* resistance to dethroning the King of Heaven. The most widely held explanation is that assaulting the maleness of God assaults male primacy and earthly patriarchal power. Mary Daly puts it this way in *Beyond God the Father* (p. 19): "If God is male, then the male is God." If the male is God-like on earth, he is literally in charge. As God is Lord of the world, so the man is lord of the manor—and the legislature, business and industry, academia, the military, the judicial system, and the church. It is easier for him to continue to be lord of the manor precisely because the authority of the powerful image he shares with God is unassailable. The authority of men becomes so taken for granted that both women and men fail to question male authority. Leadership and power become men's work. A more accurate saying than Daly's is, If God is *exclusively* male, then the male is God-like in human affairs.

Men's Authority and Autonomy

The authority of earthly men is only one of the implications of viewing God as exclusively male. Another even more sinister implication is that only men are fully human. Humans are made in the image of God. If the image of God is male, only male humans are fully human. This is not just a logical exercise, a conjecture. As early as the sixth century, the church authorities—all male—debated whether or not women had souls. The Council of Mâcon took a vote on the matter. We won. We won by one vote! That vote was taken in a historical context in which women were unapologetically viewed by the church fathers as defective men. That debate and decision were preceded by a progressive assault on the right of women to exercise leadership in the church until the Council of Laodicea (365) abolished the "ordination" of women. In short, there are ample historical data to illustrate that both humanity and authority are linked to each other as male benefits and that both are linked in turn to the maleness of God.

The feminist accusation, therefore, that men want to keep God exclusively male in order to legitimate their own earthly power is well founded. That is true enough. What's so terrific about earthly power? Happily, both men and women are now noticing the disadvantages to power. But there are still many advantages. There's money in it. Money buys prestige as well as things. Especially in the United States, where a person's worth is measured by income. The question "How much are you worth?" usually elicits a financial answer. Of the many advantages to power, one is peculiarly valued in the Western tradition, appealing as it does to the rugged individualism of the American dream.

That advantage is independence: a defense against vulnerability and a protection against involvement. Independence. Self-sufficiency. The need not to need. One of the things patriarchy does need is the persistence of the myth, the myth of male autonomy.

The displacement of God as entirely Father exposes that myth. It is exposed in a primal and ultimate way. When men keep hold of the self-sufficient, unilateral Father, they incorrectly presume the Creator's self-sufficiency—and also their own as the male mirror of the male God. If God is not entirely Father, neither is God self-sufficient and *neither are earthly men*. Women also suffer in the wake of the exposure of needy men, which is why women collaborate in keeping the myth alive. It is like facing the emperor who is without clothes. If we all pretend he is dressed, he might just as well be. None of us has to face the reality of his vulnerability. Pretense is an adequate wardrobe.

The reality is that men are not autonomous, independent, in charge, and in control. No matter how great their economic and political power—and it is great—they are dependent upon women for a kind of perpetual "mothering" in a culture and religion that values male autonomy. I can only guess what it must be like for men to acknowledge dependency, particularly the calling up of their own childish dependence. I can, however, do some informed guessing, because much of my professional experience has been a "male" mode of experience. The one vivid characteristic of that experience is aloneness. Traditional male behavior is solitary—solitary research, solitary speaking, solitary writing. All that solitariness has little to do with the virtues of solitude: It is just aloneness, because solitary behavior is often the consequence of competition between individuals for the best grade, job, or salary. For example, when most teachers say "Do your own work" they are saying much more than "Don't copy." They are saying, "Don't collaborate; don't help each other; stay alone; stay independent; teamwork is cheating." When I taught graduate

students I encouraged them to help each other in several
ways. One of those ways was collaboration in their preparation. Whenever they did share their very own "independent" work, I expected the class to say thank you and in
other ways show their appreciation, rather than rush to the
attack to show how smart they were. All of them said they
enjoyed it. But some said it still felt like cheating. The
alienating habits of individualism were that strong.

Individuality in its extreme becomes isolation. Perhaps
that is why male social systems requiring groups, such as
sports, are such highlights in a man's life. Solitariness calls
up both the need for and fear of dependence on "mother."
Mother is the one who rewards and also the one who
punishes. So the memory and need to return to her is a
mixed blessing. Even when the rewarding feelings domi-
nate, the experience of calling up mother is an infantile
experience. Of course I feel needful—yes, infantile—in
some of those alone moments too. But I am a mother
myself, and I know I can mother myself. I am not restricted to my external mother, writ large by a memory
expanded to fill expanded time. Furthermore, I can ask for
mothering from other women. I have permission to be
dependent and vulnerable. In fact, dependence and vulnerability are characteristics encouraged by the culture and
are considered virtues in women. But not in men. Men are
expected to be independent, to reach inside themselves for
nurture, affirmation, and strength. The woman takes for
granted some level of dependence on the external world
for internal growth. The man takes for granted some level
of autonomy that makes the external world gratuitous.
Men more habitually value autonomous self-affirmation.
In certain situations, their colleagueship with other men is
admirable. Dependence on women is not. A confession of
needing mothering is a weakness scorned by captains of
industry precisely because they are the captains. They are
in charge. So the solitariness in which men remember what
they have lost and what they still need must indeed be

frightening. What can they do about it? Often they deny
the need while raging against the loss. Rosemary Ruether
credibly argues (in *Witness*) that "male repression of the
mother complex" is a key to male resistance of women in
priestly functions that are "more what mothers do than
what fathers do." It must indeed be fearful to know the loss
of mothering and simultaneously to realize that you have
to develop some responsibilities for mothering yourself
when you do not know how.

Then comes the challenge to give nurturing to another.
Except for clergy, most men are neither trained nor
rewarded for any of that "mothering." Clergymen are
ambiguously rewarded, however. They are still expected to
play the autonomous male role, even as they are expected
to be available to parishioners and engage them deeply.
They are expected to exercise authority and simultaneously be the listening, nonjudgmental counselor. Many
cannot or do not acknowledge that they also need a pastor.
After all, they *are* the pastors. If clergymen received care
within "their" congregation, autonomy and authority
would be undermined. Many clergymen repress their
mothering needs and rage privately against their isolation,
just as other men do. Those clergymen who have worked
out their mother complex, not by repression and playing
autonomous father games but by genuinely entering into
"mothering" as pastor and priest, could be even angrier
resisters to clergywomen, but in my experience they are
not. They tend more toward grief. They mourn the loss of
the one workplace where men are rewarded for (so-called)
women's virtues. The tight job market and affirmative
action rhetoric make losses in that workplace very real. The
men who do share that workplace with women experience
yet another kind of loss. It is the loss of male bonding
around activities which they suspect might be more credibly accomplished by their women colleagues.

An exclusively male God, then, upholds male power and
male humanity as normative. An exclusively male God lifts

up a male model of independence. The exclusively male
God has no need for a mother or consort. The male human
counterpart mirrors humanity's myth of male autonomy
while privately confronting his frightening needs. So a
critique of God as Father is appropriate, especially as a
critique of God as exclusively male. When God as Father is
also the exclusively male God, the Father symbol is linked
with images of power, dominance, and distance alienating
to both women and men. There are, furthermore, specific
advantages to women in such a critique.

Women's Rage and Grief

The displacement of the Father symbol does have the
advantage of reducing patriarchal power over us. Humanity and authority are no longer male prerogatives. On the
other hand, that displacement also acknowledges the
unavailability of males to us. Women face the emptiness,
the aloneness, the end of hope for a reliable man. What we
mourn in God as "Parent" or "Creator" or "Mother" is the
ultimate loss of a male presence in a culture in which we
are already too much aware of his absence. We want to
keep our Father God to stave off the emptiness and
loneliness. We want the presence of a Father God to
maintain hope for a reliable presence on earth. *We want the
reliability of a Father God because we have scant experience of a
reliable man. We mourn the death of God the Father because he is
the one available Father who is reliable.*

The distinction between depending on and placing reliability in a male God is crucial here and needs to be
discussed by feminists. Traditional dependency myths say
that a man *takes care* of a woman's economic needs; a
woman *takes care* of a man's emotional needs. That kind of
caretaking rescues and controls and prevents growth and
maturity.

Ellen Willis in "The Politics of Dependency" helpfully
describes dependencies of both sexes in our culture.

Dependence, in the pejorative sense, is an infantile refusal to accept responsibility for managing one's life, for making decisions and acting on them. Dependent people adopt a helpless attitude, designed to get others to provide for their needs and/or tell them what to do. Dependence in this sense is not confined to women, but is a characteristic mode of behavior in a hierarchical society. For dominant classes the right to be dependent on others is a form of privilege, for oppressed classes a form of compensation.

Some dependent women who mourn the assault on God the Father, I suspect, do not want to acknowledge or accept responsibility for economic or emotional adulthood. Some dependent men who fear the displacement of God as Father do not want to acknowledge the indirect power of mother control, which is enraging to them, or accept mothering responsibility. Immature women and men need a controlling King of Heaven and a continuity to traditional power arrangements on earth, even while resenting the control and harboring its deep resentments. By contrast, mature women and men do not need to control or manage another's life. Nor do they need, then, a cosmic excuse for that control. Instead, they accept both economic and emotional responsibility for themselves. They share who they are with others and let go of the consequences.

Unhappily, both women and men have been so habituated to dependency relationships in our economic and political systems that appeals to maintaining infantile relationships fall on receptive ground. And one of the powerful attractions of the religious radical right is just that: rhetorical maintenance of immature power relationships. It is not only for keeping women in their place; it is also for keeping both men and women in dependency. The Moral Majority has a political package that keeps women in the home and men in the world and both of them dependent on the other for caretaking. These dependent men and women are then encouraged to be dependent upon the President—who embodies American power—with little criticism of that power or its use in foreign affairs. In this way, paternalistic and immature power relations extend to national and international as well as personal relationships. The ultimate dependency is on the powerful, paternalistic, patriarchal, unambiguous God, who is in charge and who expects obedience to him and subjection to his patriarchal representatives. The radical right capitalizes on our sorrow over the loss of the reliable Father in heaven and earth for exploitative and further alienating ends. The most danger-ous exploitation of that loss is a strong father image of the radical right preacher-man and his counterpart in Wash-ington, both of whom "know what they are doing." (What they are doing is preparing for and legitimating nuclear disaster.) But the dependent who have already given their power away to these father substitutes are impotent to perceive or prevent that.

For folks who aspire to maturity, reliability is the value. Reliable persons are just there: present, available. They mean it when they say, "I'm here. Call if you need me." They answer the phone, too. And they listen. They cannot, should not, be trusted to do whatever we ask or expect. They can, should, be trusted to be themselves with us. They cannot, should not, be counted on to tell us what we want to hear. They can, should, be counted on to tell us the truth so we can trust what we hear.

The mature have integrity. Out of that integrity comes the strength and an effortless kind of courage to be oneself with other folks. Calling out for God is something like that: knowing that someone trustworthy is always there. Reli-ability does not depend on gender. In that sense, which parent picks up the phone doesn't matter.

What does matter is that most women do not experience men with that kind of reliability.

That is why many women rage against the loss of their Father God. They are mourning the loss of the one reliable male presence in their lives. Many women express rage in response to inclusive language in worship. When they hear

"Creator" or "Sustainer" they feel robbed, cheated. Their God the Father is gone and they are furious. Often, that rage is an expression of their grief. Anger is a typical response to grief. The reality of emptiness is, among other things, enraging. They need a reliable Father God.

We should not disparage holding on to Father God out of the plain need to have one. That is one of the reasons humans choose or create images of God. That need is confirmed in many ways. *Psychology Today,* for example, reports that in one study, a majority of converts to *any religion* name the finding of a father as the most important motivation.

Jeanette Stokes reports a conversation about God language with a colleague who told of her father's death when she was eight. And then came this unsolicited comment: "Can you imagine how important God the Father is when you don't have a father?" I can. Father images in Sunday school compensated me somehow for being abandoned by my father. As a child I just *knew* there was a father somewhere. The image was and remains a sustaining one.

Patriarchal Stereotypes of God as Father

Feminist literature criticizes the use of Father images particularly for its effect on women who have scant happy experiential access to a human father. These women are more likely to attribute to that other Father the fearful alien strength of worldly power. Some pastors never use the image for this reason.

What is lost—for women as well as men—in abandoning the father symbol? What kind of father is rejected? Why?

The abandoned father symbol is, most frequently, a patriarchal stereotype. Many feminists who want to abolish God as Father want to abolish a particular kind of father image: a tyrannical one. Dorothee Soelle, for example, rejects any father language but describes the father she rejects in very specific ways. The dominant characteristic of that particular father is power. That power is expressed as aggression and is used for subjection, especially the subjection of women. As such, father language is a legitimization of the status quo, for it in fact describes the status quo. God as Father becomes "a man raised to a higher power, whose chief ideal it is to be independent and to have power" ("A Feminist Reflection"). It seems to me that this particular father is indeed a tyrant who does not exhaust even the human experience of fatherhood. Even the worst of fathers have moments of tenderness and protection. There is more to fathering than this narrow alienating definition of it. This definition is not even the projection of our best selves. Neither does this image exhaust the biblical and theological tradition. A very specific kind of father is being dismissed. That father is a masochistic distortion. We actually invest self-hating characteristics in God and worship a God who does not even like us. (Perhaps this is one reason we sometimes select men who don't like us, either.) That father is a kind of infantile neofascist, preoccupied with his power and control needs. It is the kind of father that the radical religious right tends to picture.

It is strategically inept to permit the right both to describe and own the important image. It is reminiscent of the blunder of the sixties when the peace movement people burned the flag instead of parading it. The need for father is too great to give away that easily. Its significance in the tradition is too great to erase very quickly. The symbol needs to be transformed in the tradition and in our experience. In particular, the symbol needs to be used to create a different human situation. Symbols can be change agents as well as descriptions of mundane history.

There is danger in using the symbol in too inverted a way, by projecting onto Father God the *experience* of loss rather than the *wisdom* of loss. The former projection is indeed alien and static, and it is better to let go of the Father altogether than to project in him our loss. That kind of a symbol becomes remote and unavailable. He is more a statement of the problem than a solution. The problem is enlarged and becomes grotesque among those who combine fearful images such as Wholly Other, Omnipotent, Judge, and Avenger and add these to Absent Father. Religion becomes a divine reign of terror.

There is another danger in defining the content of father. That danger is depositing onto the Father the romanticized presence of an earthly man. In such an instance, the Father God serves as an escape from the reality of one's earthly relationships—a mere distraction and pretense, a romantic fantasy. Some women fall in love with God, marry the church, and withdraw from engaging earthly men to avoid disappointment. I do not mean to reject either celibacy or a primary calling to a church vocation. There are many Christian women who are healthy, centered celibates, and that health may very well include mature relationships with men. There are also plenty of Christian women who confess that celibacy is a defense or that the church is a protective place. For these women a love affair with God is not a metaphor for intimacy. For these women it is an antiseptic fantasy of intimacy, which defends against the touching of the world. It is untouched and unworldly. We can spiritualize the whole range of our sexual relationships just as the radical right spiritualizes the Gospel, with the same result: a failure to take responsibility for reality. In our case it is specifically a failure to insist that men take responsibility for themselves and for fathering. In this scenario, the Father is another status quo symbol, for we have made no strategic connection between the God image and a human reality. Or—worse—sometimes we just pretend the connection already exists and there is no need for changing the human sexual arrangements.

This escape from facing a future of sexual relationships may be the refusal to see to it that there is a future at all. There are those who argue that the fathering of children is a sheer survival issue. Fathers must engage in the work of caring for their children so that fathers have an intimate involvement in their children's future—and therefore an involvement in seeing to it that there is a future for all the children of the next generation. Now that the fathers in Washington and other capitals talk of the viability of nuclear conflict, real fathering is a survival strategy. Dorothy Dinnerstein is one of the most persuasive advocates of this. Consequently, theological naming that romanticizes the Father God is not just an escape from a disappointing personal present. It can be also an escape from the hard work of building a life-affirming collective future.

Fortunately, God is God, apart from our images. Fortunately, escape is hard to come by. "Getting free of Father God may be as hard as getting free of our own parents" (Jean Caffey Lyles). Exactly. Parents are so omnipresent in the human experience, and familial relationships are so significant, it would be remarkable not to associate the Creator with human procreation. For that reason, feminists who want to be free of the Father symbol will continue to face extreme resistance. But father is only one of the parents. He is, furthermore, the less compelling parent in the creation story, the center-stage drama of which is birthing. That is clearly the mother's job.

God as Goddess

What, then, of the Mother God? If mothers are most often experienced as reliable, the Mother God calls up that kind of strength. She can be for us a symbol of cosmic comfort because she will respond to our needs. Sally Gearhart concludes that we *cannot* expect men as a gender to shift into providing nurture. The existing socialization is just too immense. This suggests to her that the female *must* be the figure of cosmic quest and response. Much feminist theology claims and reclaims Goddess images, or reclaims the mothering of the biblical God, or both.

Some appropriate a wide variety of feminine images. Some are biblical, some are not. Rita Gross, for example, looks at Goddess images in Hindu literature. She does not believe that the presence of goddesses necessarily represents a historical fact of an equality or superiority of women. In that sense, a Goddess does not now help promote equality. Gross persuasively argues, however, that the sheer expression of divinity in *any* female form does promote women as created in the image of God. When divinity is represented as male, the maleness becomes normative for humanity. If women participate in the image of *that* God at all, we do so only partially, defectively, or occasionally. Female symbols for God are essential to maintaining the fullness of the image of God for women. That essential connection is logically and historically demonstrable. I agree that the connection must be made between the female image of God and the image of God in females. Furthermore, I believe that this image of God indirectly promotes equality also through the development of a stronger self-image. When I image myself as God-like, I have an internal affirmation of worth and dignity. That stronger self-image can in turn make it easier to satisfy my needs and promote my rights. For the fullness of the image of God and the promotion of equality, Goddess images are essential. Mother is one of those Goddess images in both the Hindu and Christian tradition. She needs to be reclaimed, with some caution. The caution is that birthing and nurturing need to be affirmed, *without* confining women to these historical tasks. Gross's ideal god image is bisexual: the androgynous Mother and Father. There are the characteristics of both men and women in one God. That androgynous ideal is the same for most feminist Christians, who are more likely to use the resources of Scripture to demonstrate that androgyny.

Feminists have been hard pressed to use the resources of Scripture, androgynous or otherwise. One reason for that is that some of the liberating beliefs and practices of the early church have been obscured and suppressed. Whenever Bible translators use the generic masculine, the exclusion of women can be projected onto the early church. Whenever the life situations of the early church are ignored, texts can become isolated rules. Whenever intervening history is ignored, uncouth truths of ancients get stuck into our contemporary time and space. God as Mother was suppressed by the tradition.

Elaine Pagels is one who describes some historical politics of that suppression. She exposes a part of early Christianity as gnostic communities that used both male and female images, who prayed to the Father and Mother, and whose Trinity was Father-Mother-Son. Women participated in the leadership of these communities. These views were forced outside the church by the end of the second century by those who insisted upon an exclusively male leadership both in heaven and on earth. Then the winners set about to write the history. The winners called themselves "orthodox." They called the losers "heretics."

The kind of research done by Pagels opens up the Scripture and the tradition to feminist theologians and helps us appropriate both as our own in at least three ways: (1) It adds to the body of evidence which places the Scriptures into the historical context, reminding us that part of the early church made decisions as to what we would read as authoritative; (2) that awareness in turn provokes fresh insight into the Scriptures; and (3) the Jesus movement is rediscovered as more inclusive and more radical than the church would like us to believe. The "orthodox" party—who decided what we should know—worshiped an exclusively male God. It is remarkable that *any* feminine imagery survived the preaching and teaching of the church.

Religion, Rebellion, and Reliability

As the early "orthodox" among Christians adhered to an exclusively male god, so some contemporary feminists adhere to an exclusively female god. There is an emerging religious consciousness, sometimes called womanspirit religion or revolutionary religion or countercultural religion, which concentrates on female images and experience. Theologians such as Carol Christ have intentionally separated themselves from a Judeo-Christian tradition viewed as hopelessly partriarchal. Carol Christ's own journey began as a participant in the Judaic Christian communities. She saw the central symbol system—God as Father and Jesus as the Christ—as the core of religion, and she assessed that core as inescapably and exclusively masculine.

The emerging consciousness concentrates on women's experiences as primary data for religious reflection and community. Those religious communities include women's house churches and witches' covens. Many of the womanspirit theologians believe in an original matriarchal culture presided over by the Mother Goddess. So there is a sense of recovery of an ancient, prepatriarchal religious symbol precious in the lives of women. To whatever extent an ancient goddess is recalled or recovered, there are currently Mother Goddess symbols available to much of the womanspirit religion. That contemporary Mother Goddess is connected to the earth and all things natural.

Womanspirit religion can be criticized as duplicating some of the errors of patriarchal religion. It runs the danger of elitism. My Goddess is better than your God. My experience is better than your experience. Explicit or implicit separatism is a similar danger. Women know we do not have the means to control institutions and communities populated by men. Perhaps that is one of the reasons womanspirit religion separates instead of trying to take over the tradition as the "orthodox" party did. Perhaps another reason is not to be contaminated. I believe there is an additional motivation. It is this.

There is the dynamic of such profound disappointment in the Father symbols as to make it necessary to recover exclusive Mother symbols. Some of that genre, in fact, reads more like rebellion against male authority than the recovery of women's spirituality. Naomi Goldenberg, for example, calls us to leave patriarchal power behind and come into our own power, which is presented by "rebels" such as witches. She then refers to God and Christ as reminders of "patriarchal" monotheism which we have "*outgrown*" (italics mine). Sometimes womanspirit religion declares utter independence and asserts that there are no gods with objective reality or power external to oneself. Goldenberg is one who completes this rebellion against the father, believing we will (again) "*outgrow* the need for an external god." She argues that everyone turns inward when the father is *lost* and notes the *distant* father and *available* mother in our culture (italics mine). In short, it is *precisely* the search for reliability that is a motivation for womanspirit religion.

The rebellion against male religion and the utter determination to place confidence and authority within oneself feels like the protective speech of the disappointed and injured: "Never again. I will not take a chance. I will come back to myself and those like me. I will cling to my mother, the one I can trust." I believe that somewhere in the core of this consciousness is the search for reliability in the Goddess and even more for reliability in oneself. The development of a religious consciousness that rebels against a dependency on the father and looks to the exclusive or primary control of the mother is very much like the same dynamic of disappointment, grief, and rage of women who have lost their Father at Sunday morning worship. The behavior, of course, is utterly different. Womanspirit behavior is to cling to the experience of the reliable mother in the form of the goddess within, and if the distant father is permitted reentry at all, he is in a subordinate, peripheral, or combative place. The combat is a kind of protest, and protests are dependent upon the "enemy" for sustenance. Insofar as separation from father is a protest, it is still dependent upon the father and has only a shadow life, without an independent content of its own.

Then there is the danger of exchanging a dependence on father for a dependence on nature. It is a curious thing that a consciousness which so reacts against one dependency and so longs for independence is willing to entertain a dependency on nature, which has its own history of capricious, arbitrary, and dangerous behavior. I do not wonder why mother is more reliable and more attractive. I do wonder why much of womanspirit religion should accept an essentially patriarchal view of the feminine which centers on motherhood tied to nature.

There is a curious kind of rediscovery of female nature throughout the women's movement and the culture, which romanticizes women's birthing and nursing capabilities. Often those biological capabilities are extended into the social world, so that "real" women are nurturers and enablers. Hence, women's behavior is held up as "different," and different is restrictive. This is nothing new. Biological determinism has a long tradition as a way of keeping women in their place. That feminists hold up this restrictive model for women is also not new. Many of the participants in the first wave of the movement held on to a restrictive view of women. A key argument for educating women was to improve their role as mothers. A key argument for the franchise was to improve the body politic by the "nobler" sex. In short, much of the first wave of feminism had the effect of reinforcing roles and stereotypes of women. The Motherhood of God was rediscovered also during the first wave of the movement. For example, in 1901 a Louis Banks published a book titled *The Motherhood of God*. This is his commentary on Isaiah 66:13 ("As one whom his mother comforts, so I will comfort you"): "Come pillow your head here and find forgiveness." He goes on:

The man who does not believe in vicarious atonement does not know much about how mothers give themselves for their children.

Here is Mother Comfort, a one-dimensional woman, whose bosom receives patriarchal sorrow (and punishment?). The resurgence of women's special nature tied to nature symbolized in Mother Goddess is dangerous to women. It can more easily capture us into one stereotypical model than release us for the fullest measure and complexity of our humanity. Finally, there are dangers from limiting religious content inside one's experience, without any data located in another, in a God, the transcendent one. Insofar as the goddess is only immanent and not transcendent, there is the danger of establishing the individual person as the religious center. Women may not historically have been long on pride, but we are not immune from exaggerated pride, either. I understand transcendence as essential to religious belief. I wonder why that part of a movement that is not transcendent calls itself religious at all, but then we can name our consciousness anything we wish. Perhaps the *collective* wisdom is in some sense a transcendence to the *individual* self. It is surely true that we stretch and grow partly as we are helped by others.

I find the preoccupation with women's experience helpful. Methodologically, what any of us has is experience from which to make inferences, about the world and about gods. Perhaps there is a need in most of us at one time or another in our spiritual development to start over, reach into the recesses of our own experience, and distance ourselves from whatever mythology has shaped us. Bible-quoting feminists do that too. Women's experience provides new provocative data for a wide range of theologies. Womanspirit feminists both remind us of the importance of that enterprise and provide more of the data based on women's experience.

The danger is that the experience will remain existential

and neither be connected up with the vastness of women's experience into a larger analysis nor be related to men's experience, except as men are perceived as different or "the other," "the enemy." An existential consciousness prevents pressing toward spiritual resolution in at least two very different ways. First, the existential data of women's experience stand over against God as Father and over against male experience. That "over-against-ness" can temporarily escape conflict in the sheer withdrawal from a male world. Or it can provoke more conflict as distinctions between male and female are drawn. But an existential consciousness cannot and will not ultimately relieve the sorrow and rage. Neither will it heal the alienation between the sexes. Second, the data are too scattered, independent, and separate to survive very long in their present form. I think of two very practical examples of what this means.

The first example has to do with conversations with women in Mexico. Several feminists told me about projects that covered a wide variety of activities and goals. Included were establishing caucuses within labor unions, organizing specific women's trades into labor unions, educating rural women, initiating theological reflections and actions within the church, developing coalitions around specific issues, and developing a political power base. On two separate occasions, two different women told me about two different, short-lived women's organizations with almost an identical analysis. They both said that the organization was too existential to survive. I inquired further to be sure I understood their meaning. Each went on to say that those particular women were too concerned about their own personal experience and individual development to use those insights for a broad-based political purpose and constituency. The explanations were what I suspected. I believe that *any* branch or brand of feminism that does not engage a larger community and that does not move into political activity is an endangered species. Some woman-

spirit religion eschews the very kind of worldly power that
could keep it alive.

A second example is provided by Elaine Pagels. Why was
it that the early church rejected the gnostic communities
that were so hospitable to women? How was the church
able to suppress the history of gnosticism so that their
models became only partially accessible to us? Partly because the gnostics were *elitists* who claimed a special spirituality, whereas the "orthodox leaders attempted instead
to construct a *universal* church." Gnostics who resisted
organization "survived, as churches, for only a few hun-
dred years." Our gnostic ancestors had not only the right
but the wisdom to resist the particulars of that ecclesiastical
organization. One of those particulars worth resisting was
the patriarchal model of highly authoritative individual
bishops. Nevertheless, I wonder "what might have been"
had that resistance been mounted inside the organization
and had their special spiritual experience been shared
more than protected. I wonder, too, what the connection is
between the universal church and the universality of mind
that makes both attractive. Could our Mother have survived as more than a suppressed shadow of the feminine?

Of course, there is no way to know. Nor do we yet know
the impact and disposition of womanspirit religion. It is
entirely possible, however, that insofar as womanspirit
religion's *special spirituality* resists the so-called male characteristics, including organization and political activity, it
too could wither away. We would then lose a contribution
to consciousness and a source for change. We would lose
the powerful exploration of particular women's experiences and images of the divine Mother. We would lose
touch with the Mother God who comforts and empowers
us. She gives us a home in the world and in the church. She
gives us a staying power because we know her as the one
who will stay there for us. She is a symbol of reliability most
of us have learned at our mother's knee.

Yet it is precisely because our earthly mothers are

reliable that loss of the Father God is so great. The Goddess by herself accentuates separation, alienation, and mourning. I do not abandon the Mother God. I need her. But I hold on to God the Father too. The mythical throne I look to is shared, a source of inspiration for shared parenting and healing of alienations between the sexes. At least one of our mothers, Mary Baker Eddy, made the connection between the "illness" of society-induced alienations and the healing symbols of Mother-Father-God. Eddy knew firsthand the alienation of the sexes. Eddy's Christian Science holds up the symbols of both parents as necessary for God-centered healing.

God as Neither Mother nor Father

We can, of course, set a high value on sharing and healing without using parent language at all. In fact, some argue that parent language helps to keep us children. The argument continues: As children, we are in a one-down position because each parent represents someone bigger and stronger. So the power is still attributed to someone else, outside the self. This is not healthy for anybody; it is especially unhealthy for women. We need to develop our own power, not give it away. Soelle, for example, prefers to use mystical language and to find God in brothers and sisters because these are images of equity.

First of all, to state the obvious: Most men who have used the symbol of Father have not emptied themselves of power. There is, therefore, no necessary connection between the use of parent language and the giving away of one's power. I suspect parent language is not the big issue. "Father" is the big issue. Since "Father" won't do, parenting won't do. What about the notion that parent language keeps us in childhood and restricts our power? Parent power has the advantage, especially in the early years, of focusing on the acceptance, love, patience, and sacrifice necessary to a child's survival and critical to a child's sense of safety, growth, risk, and discovery. Furthermore, the argument about power refers to a very limited vision of parenting as especially concentrated on a (temporary) power advantage. Competent parents encourage independent decision-making with the growth of the offspring. As parents age, the middle-aged "kids" are increasingly in charge. Somewhere in between there is a rough kind of equity. We forget that development toward equity partly because this is precisely the time in life when families are expected to separate. We have this bizarre ideal of parents and children being together when children are young and exhausting and then again when parents are infirm and depressing. During the time when they could enjoy each other, it is a mark of maturity for the young folks to leave town and for everybody to grieve through the best years. At any rate, parenting is not static. Neither does it end when the children achieve legal or financial parity. In some stages and some situations there is equity. In others, there are power imbalances. In all stages, furthermore, there is much more to the relationships than the balance of power.

Parents are too omnipresent and too significant in the experience of humankind to be exorcised from religious imagination and symbols. A more appropriate and helpful theological task is to transform parent language for God. Transformation of that parent language includes using mother language. Transformation also includes using father language that is relational and reliable. Reliable father language is difficult to come by in our culture and in our time. The reason for that is that men are experienced as unreliable.

2

Absence
of Modern Men

Men are experienced as unreliable because our most typical experience of them, especially fathers, is the experience of absence. What is absent is the comfortable presence of a man who engages a woman with his feelings and relates to her as a partner and friend. They are absent in at least five ways: (1) They are just gone because of work patterns, (2) they are absent through abandonment or an occasional presence, (3) they are absent as an anticipated presence, (4) they are emotionally absent, or (5) they are absent as fathers by being physically present and dangerous.

Work Patterns

Fathers are just gone because of employment patterns, which have not substantially changed despite the dramatic increase of mothers in the paid labor force. There are several ways in which these employment patterns contribute to our experience of absence.

First of all, the well-paid prestigious jobs are usually men's jobs, and they take enormous amounts of time. For example, most industry still expects the successful worker to owe his primary allegiance to the company. One of the things this means is a very time-consuming job away from home. That more than full-time job away from the family

could often be done in much less time. There is a kind of
mystique about "overwork" that has more to do with male
bonding, loyalty to the company, and self-identification
than it has to do with the requirements of production.
Think about it. "Successful" businessmen sit on decision-
making boards within the community. They are guest
speakers for this and that. How is it that they have the
time? One of the reasons for "overwork" is that sheer
weariness of spending too many hours on the job makes
those hours on the job inefficient. Another is the need to
prove commitment. Still another is that these men literally
don't know what else to do with themselves.

I still remember vividly my first on-the-job meeting
twenty-five years ago. That was the beginning of the
comical realization that *whatever* men did at work was
considered important. I was the sole female, young, in-
experienced, and eager. I sat through a long meeting,
yellow pad in hand. When the meeting was over, there was
nothing written on that pad. I felt terrible. Surely I had
missed something important. There was something wrong
with me. It was *years* before I realized there was, in fact,
nothing of sufficient importance to record. Lest we be too
hard on the individual worker, however, we must acknowledge that employers conspire to keep workers away from
home. I taught a class of women several years ago. All of
them were middle-aged. Most of them were married to
"successful" business and professional men. One of those
women brought to class a remarkable document. She had
stolen a memorandum from her husband's briefcase. The
memo advised the company's managers on the obligations
of company wives. It included some predictable activities,
such as being a proper hostess. But this memo also gave the
husband arguments to use at home as to why he could not
be there more and *why she should not trouble him* about the
home situation! I wonder what that memo looks like today.
I suspect it is no longer written down.

Some fathers refuse the pressure to climb the ladder of

success. They are frequently punished by their company as lacking ambition and snubbed by their peers as wimps. Clearly, the workplace itself has to be changed in order for fathers to father. A twenty- to thirty-hour week must become a respectable workload. Benefits must become part of the "part-time" package. Some governmental agencies and a few businesses have demonstrated success in such alternative work patterns as job sharing, where two people fill one "full-time" position. Nearly all these alternatives require *less time on the job.* That is a high wall for bearers of the American dream to scale. The excessive hours expected of professionals and managers place particular American dream burdens on the middle class. Every one of these jobs was designed for the full-time energies of two people: the employee and his wife. Unless the hours are reduced, neither mother nor father will do much parenting. They will cope, somehow, with their four or more jobs: two shifts at the office, one additional full-time job, and home management and parenting. When that cumulative load of responsibility is added up, and the weariness and stresses set in, the children may prefer that Dad does stay away rather than displace some of his tension on them.

Second, we are increasingly aware that the "traditional" unwritten economic contract between wife and husband is unreliable. In that contract, he provides the money and she provides the support services. The economically dependent woman has been in a minority since 1974. Most married women today make money as well as babies, and those who earn little or nothing are increasingly aware of the early feminist truth, "You're just one man away from welfare." This is why battered mothers with negligible earning power "forgive" too much. I remember a young woman who sat next to me on a flight between Dallas and Atlanta. I soon discovered that she was a caseworker who dealt exclusively with battered women. She was on her way to see her fiancé for the purpose of making wedding plans. She volunteered the information that many of her clients had had happy engagements with no inkling of the later disaster of marriage. I asked her about money. "How many of your clients stay in that situation primarily for economic reasons?" Almost immediately she said, "Oh, ninety percent." Then she furrowed her brow in thought, "No," she said. "That's not true. It's closer to ninety-five percent."

Black women know better than any others that women are not exempt from economic cares. Under the press of the civil rights movement of the sixties, jobs and training programs were opened up to Black America. A 1970 statistical analysis from the Department of Labor verifies this fact. Many Black men who were economic heads of households moved up out of the poverty class. Guess what? Black women heads of households entered the poverty class in almost exactly the same proportion as the Black men leaving it. For most Black women, facing survival responsibilities in the world is not a significant loss, but it is a significant disappointment.

Women who have contracted to be economically dependent in return for wifely services have learned that those contracts can be easily broken, particularly through desertion and divorce. For poor women, the contract itself is empty. Men are in fact economically dependent upon women for necessary services or income or both.

But even though we "know" this, it is hard to acknowledge because of our precariousness in an economically hostile world. Contrary to popular mythology, the economic situation has not improved for women. Women still occupy few of the professional and managerial jobs that require the hours, travel, and intensity of career focus. We still provide the pink-collar labor force, share line-production work, and provide marginal labor, particularly in the service industry. Although more than half of us are now in the labor force, we earn 59 cents for every male-earned dollar. The gap in earning within similar job categories has actually grown since the advent of the women's movement. The one exception is among the professions, where the gap has decreased by about 2 percent. Poverty trends are alarming. Since 1967 the rate of increase of women economic heads of households is so great, sociologist Diana Pearce names it "the feminization of poverty." What that means is this: Current trends projected to the year 2000 suggest that 100 percent of the economic heads of poverty households will be women. If there are no dramatic interventions into economic and family support systems, every single poor person responsible for the care of self and others will be female.

Much of the increase in that trend is provided by single mothers. A majority of those mothers can expect only negligible child support from fathers. They can also expect more and more unskilled minimum-wage jobs to be available to them. Child-care assistance, however, is rarely available. The United States is the only industrialized western nation that does not have a child-care policy. When women who have received economic assistance from husbands are thrown back entirely on their own resources and resourcefulness, they experience still other kinds of absence in the workplace. They experience the absence of employment opportunities and the absence of child-care alternatives. They are disappointed anew by the unreliability of the men who manage the workplace and government, as neither money nor additional parenting is available to them.

Women are increasingly the working poor who confront unreliability in the workplace and at home. What about the children of two-parent families? What is the experience of those women and children? The primary professional tracks for women, such as teaching and nursing, provide the flexibility of hours that makes mothering possible. That is not an accident. When two parents are employed—even in similar jobs—mother is still the parent. This is just as true for clergy couples, the "co-mothers," as anybody else. Many of these couples report the press of the congregation to keep him as the real minister and her as the real parent.

One of these clergywomen told me of her decision to change her employment situation so that she could spend more time with her preschool children. She repeatedly told me that *she* wanted to do this *for herself*. She wanted to make it very plain that she was not reacting to pressure from congregation or family or friends. That she had to tell me that at all is evidence of the typical views of her parishioners. Those views made her task of sorting out what she wanted for herself more complex. The task was also more conflictual than it was for her husband.

Some corporations have organized flex-time schedules and rotating shifts on the production line at least partly to accommodate mothers for parenting and home management. One vice-president laments this double duty of mothers. He has, for example, staff to help couples deal with their work patterns and home obligations. He also faces the reality that in his experience most fathers will not change shifts. So the company shifts are arranged to give some coping support to mothers. His experience is verified by Susan Strasser's *Never Done: A History of American Housework*. Strasser describes changes in hours, tools, and kinds of work. One thing has not changed, a generation after the advent of the second wave of the women's movement. Women are still the domestic managers. We may receive "help" for "our" work from other members of the family, but it is our work. So we cope.

Mothers' coping and fathers' absenteeism go together. The pattern will continue as long as we throw couples back onto their own resources and expect individual solutions. The media have an abundant supply of those creative, individual solutions for the two employed parents. My impression of most of them goes something like this: She's a writer. He's an artist. They have one child. That child was born when Mom and Dad were in their thirties. Mom and Dad are financially comfortable. They live in a renovated house that is large enough to accommodate a study and a studio. They can both work at home. They live down the block from the perfect at-home grandmother. They have a full-time maid. If this is the solution, what was the problem?!

There are people who manage without this exaggerated amount of support and convenient career matches. Margaret White describes some of them in her book *Sharing Caring.* Those particular parents were committed to shared parenting from the beginning and set about ways to "work it out." Moreover, they had more opportunities to do this than most parents have. For example, most of them were in professions where some flexibility is possible. Several worked part time, one as little as ten hours a week. Yet these parents suffered doubts and stresses also. Their commitment was set over against prevailing economic and social values. Two people should not have to "work it out" in a society that restricts rewards to production and forty- to eighty-hour weeks outside the home. But they are expected to do just that.

These are some of the ways work patterns in the paid labor force and in the home contribute to the absence of fathers: more than full-time jobs for men, the decline of the traditional economic contract between husbands and wives, the singular responsibility of mothers for parenting, and the lack of money and child-care alternatives for women.

Abandonment and the Occasional Father

Fathers are even more obviously absent in most cases of abandonment and custody. Mothers still represent 90 percent of single parents.

Death of a spouse is less likely to be followed by remarriage of mothers than by remarriage of fathers. In short, fathers are often just not there. Sometimes the literal absence becomes more awesome because the whereabouts of the father is unknown. Thomas J. Cottle describes a little girl who developed fainting spells, fatigue, and nightmares precisely because her father left suddenly and she did not know what happened to him. She was not even sure whether he was dead or alive. She believed him dead, inferring this partly from the silence of relatives. When she discovered he was alive, she discovered some other unhappy truths, one of which was that he did not want to see her. Furthermore, she was not supposed to tell anybody that he was alive. The little girl was rejected, confused, and frightened. No wonder she had nightmares. She was also isolated by a conspiracy of silence from her "adult" world. This may be an atypical collection of details. It is not so unusual a situation, however.

Many children do not hear from their father after he leaves. Even if their mother or another relative knows his whereabouts, there may be no talk about it in the presence of the children. There are many "reasons" for such conspiracies of silence. One of them is that adults just see no point in talking. It's over. There is no more contact. There is no information to report. The rest of the family is getting on with their lives. Mother is in fact the only parenting parent. Her friends probably encourage her to "start over"; "Don't live in the past"; "Living well is the best revenge." So even a relatively intelligent mother can unwittingly participate in a screaming silence. She knows she is the only parent left. Unfortunately, she frequently makes too much out of this rather obvious fact. For example, because she is the only parent *present,* she may come to believe she is the only parent, period. If she is the only parent, then she is the only parent who influences the children. She may literally forget that there is another parent and that this other parent has *enormous* influence. The absent father becomes more appealing and more wanted. He also becomes a powerful model for boys. His sons may mimic him, especially in distancing themselves from Mother. Or they may rebel in their rage and punish him for leaving them by never meeting his expectations or fulfilling any of his hopes and dreams. Contrariness to the absent father can also be simply motivated: "I trusted you and you betrayed me. I cannot trust anything you represent. I will never be like you." Absence is in itself, then, a powerful influence. The mother cannot ignore it. Neither can she compensate for it.

She cannot fill the vacuum or take solitary responsibility for the children in that environment. For sanity's sake she had better hold off the temptation to be totally responsible. Mothers have been held totally responsible by every patriarchal structure from politics to pediatrics. It is ironic that it is so easy for us to do this to ourselves.

Even when the children know the whereabouts of the disappeared father, what meaning does Butte, Montana, have for a six-year-old who has never left the Bronx? Dad might just as well be on Mars. When my son learned that his father was moving to New York, he wanted to know an exact address and phone number right that minute. It was not possible to give him an address or phone number right that minute, but I assured him several times he would have that information soon. He could not be comforted. His need to locate his father was so great that he went to the address book and wrote down the scant amount of information he did have: *Dad—New York City*. My son was well beyond the conceptual and geographical limitations of the average six-year-old. He had been in New York City several times; it was neither Butte nor Mars to him. There was little mystery in the move. Imagine the awesomeness of the disappearance of a father for whom there is no location.

One of my clues as to how profound an emptiness this must be was the experience of my hurting son, who wrote *Dad—New York City*. A second clue came from listening to a woman from Argentina whose entire family except for one grandson was missing. Her government had developed a systematic way of seeing to it that persons just disappeared. It was one of the intentional tactics of terror designed to maintain power. There is a whole collection of human beings, who are referred to by loved ones who never know what happened to them as "the disappeared." The Argentine grandmother was also a professional in the medical community with a specialization in psychological trauma and disorders. She described the effects of the phenomenon of the disappeared on the children: insomnia, suspicion of all adults, inability to explore, learning disabilities, guilt, identity confusion, various fear symptoms, and social alienation. In what ways do our children know their unreachable fathers as "the disappeared"? From what fears and alienations do they suffer? What are the effects on their medical and social history?

An Anticipated Presence

A third related absence is the anticipated (but not actual) presence of the father. Mother reminds daughter that he is in the family by explaining or apologizing for his absence. Too often the explanations carry with them the threat of that mythological autonomous power. The classic example is, "Just wait till your father gets home." No self-respecting kid will sit around until that happens. Sometimes there is a positive anticipation. Oh, good. Soon Daddy will be home. This is like waiting to open the birthday present only to find socks and underwear. Dad cannot possibly fill an anticipated presence with an occasional trumpeted appearance. The occasional father knows it, too. Somewhere underneath his determined cheerfulness at the start of the annual family vacation waits the realization that it is not enough. Further, he does not have the sheer experience of developing parental habits and skills. For example, he may be unaccustomed to exercising much patience. The family vacation is one of those times when he wants desperately to be available to the children and may not. For they can press beyond his limits of patience. Then he becomes the wielder of power, the fearful one, at exactly the time the children's expectations—and his—are happiest. Disappointment is

shared by all. The occasional father is predictably disappointing.

Emotional Absence

That brings us to another kind of absence, the fathers
who are physically present and emotionally absent. The
institution of fatherhood is still related to power relationships in the world in which he has rights. He has also
certain concomitant rights in the family. One of these is the
right to receive emotional services from the children's
mother just as the children do. One of the factors in the
emotionally absent father is that he expects to receive
emotional support as something rightfully his. He does not
expect to give it. Those expectations provide him with little
motivation to develop emotional competencies. Emotional
services become women's work. The emotionally absent
father is much more anxious about his situation than either
he or the culture admits. David White provides some clues
that fathers are at least more concerned about emotional
closeness with children than they were a generation ago. I
suspect they are simply somewhat more willing to confess
it. The anxiety of emotional isolation is immense. First of
all, what his children's mother gives she can take away.
Adrienne Rich, after reviewing some of the legal decisions
surrounding divorce, custody, and paternal kidnapping,
credibly argues:

> Much male fear of feminism is the fear that, in becoming whole
> human beings, women will cease to mother men, to provide the
> breast, the lullaby, the continuous attention associated by the
> infant with the mother. [That fear] is infantilism . . . arrested
> development.

But that fear is not only a case of arrested development.
This analysis of the situation is much too imbalanced.

A second anxiety emerges out of the realization that he
has not been trained for that kind of job. He does not know

how to be emotionally present. How could he have learned it? The model for manhood that he learned at home is the tough, controlled, distant man of the world, reinforced by the Idealized Man of his culture. That Idealized Man wears uniforms: white coats, military insignia, business suits, hard hats, or clerical collars. He gives orders: scalpel, march, take a memo, check the specs, God says. The Idealized Man is the autonomous man who "matures" in separation from others. The little boy hears early the twin admonitions "Men don't cry" and "Be a man." So he learns to stifle the tears *and the feelings behind them.* How can he function in that kind of world? By hiding and then numbing the feelings. After a while, he literally does not feel. By contrast, emotional presence requires vulnerability, the sharing of fears and confessing of errors, the nurturing skills of listening, observing, touching. Deep from his childhood memory is the elusive longing for these things. But they were stolen from him, assigned to his mother and sisters. Now as an adult he knows his limits and doesn't know what to do about it. The emotionally absent father could be particularly afraid of the loss of mothering because it is his one connection to the emotional world.

Dangerous Fathers

Finally, the absence of fathering also is experienced in the physically dangerous presence. Fathers are the major source of child abuse and 95 percent of the source of sexual abuse. They are frightening. (It is worth noting that the inclusive language of "domestic violence" and "child abuse" was easy to come by in situations where the female is the primary victim of male violence.) According to the Center of Child Abuse and Neglect, the number of cases of sexual abuse is at least 100,000 a year. That is the most conservative estimate available. Other estimates range as high as 500,000 a year. As many as one out of every three girls is a victim of sexual abuse. Just as adult women are the

objects of pornography and rape, so little girls experience
a special vulnerability to incest and the rapidly growing
kiddie porn industry. Incest does include a wide range of
sexual activity by different members of the family, but the
coercion of daughters by fathers and father figures is the
most common.

Daughters carry, then, a heavy load of sexual abuse as
well as their share of child abuse. And daughters carry that
weight mostly from fathers. Many of those abused daughters observe the battering of their mothers. We now know
that wife abusers are indeed more likely to abuse children
also. So abused daughters learn at least two frightening
lessons.

First, they learn to associate their gender with victimization. Often, they learn that victimization has a kind of
"normalcy" to it. We know that many children are victims
from incredibly early ages. Some of them are literally
abused in the cradle. They are reared with abuse and the
expectation of abuse. Because of their isolation, they come
to believe that abuse is normative just as their family's
selection of certain kinds of food, music, chores, and
entertainment is normative. Furthermore, they learn that
they are somehow responsible. Girls are told they will be in
trouble if they break the silence. And, indeed, they are. I
have heard adults ask why a girl *allowed* something to
happen, as if a powerless, isolated child had the resources
to make a choice!

Second, daughters learn to associate men, especially
fathers, with power and danger. They are very aware of
their own powerlessness, which is also normative in that
family structure and history. There are very limited ways
of escaping or preventing the danger. One of them is to
limit the danger by contracting with the father figure to be
available to him if he will leave the other siblings alone. In
this way, the girl is reinforced in the larger message of
being a caretaker for others at her own expense. So it is
that daughters associate victimization with themselves and

associate power and danger with fathers, even as they wistfully long for a change in the father figure to *return* to them as a loving parent.

There we have it: at least five ways to experience the absence of fathering. When I first described these absences in a 1981 article, many women told me, Yes, that was indeed their experience. I was not surprised by their stories of confirmation. What did surprise me was some of the expressions of grief. There were tears and reports of tears. A few reported grieving openly for the first time. The mourning was hidden and deep. Confronting the absence is an experience in unreliability that opens up disappointment and grief. Grief is transmitted into rage. Some of that rage is displaced against the loss of God the Father.

The Oddity of Emotionally Present Men

There are those blessed fathers who in spite of and in the midst of patriarchy try to be healthfully present. There is little support from friends. There are few living examples of how to do this. Our institutions still throw those fathers back on their individual resources and solutions, which is one of the causes for their absence, especially emotional absence, in the first place. Men are isolated from each other as fathers. They are expected to gather for work and recreation, but not for parenting. They are encouraged to leave their personal life at home. The minority of caring fathers who do turn out for the PTA or conferences with teachers sit miserably in the little chairs listening to the women experts.

Some men have taken the clue from the women's movement and formed their own support groups to discover what their priorities really are, apart from the definitions handed to them from the culture. Some of them take on the awesome task of learning how to be emotionally present to their children. They practice confessing errors, partly so that their children can feel safe and accepted in particular failures. They cuddle and comfort. They say, "I love you." When they leave work and show up at the Emergency Room, the children believe it too. They ask the children how they feel and what they want. They accept deviant career plans. These fathers are working against the signals and structures. As good as they are for their daughters, they are also peculiar. Media messages tell us that things are working out, whether it is a news report or a film fantasy like *Kramer vs. Kramer,* which congratulates a man for what a woman takes for granted. The reality is otherwise. In fact, the number of single fathers with custody declined in the seventies. Furthermore, the escalating divorce and remarriage patterns by fathers of minor children suggest more of the same: gone. Gone to the next wife's children, who have also lost their father. The temporariness of fatherhood is not lost on either set of offspring.

Fathers' relationships to daughters are: absent through work patterns, absent through abandonment or an occasional presence, absent with an anticipated presence, present and emotionally absent, present and dangerous, fully present and odd. This is the predicament in which we find ourselves, and which makes God as Father such an object of wistfulness. These are the amazing choices set over against the reliability of God as Father.

3

Women's
Special Compensations
and Temptations

In the face of these amazing choices, it does not take long for the daughter to discover that mothers are the reliable ones. A daughter hopes for gratification through an adult relationship with an adult male, but not until she has it does she discover that she, like her mother, is giving more intimacy than she is receiving. Daughters who look for a father substitute and find frustration can be matched with men who want to be children, or lovers, but seldom fathers. Or daughters learn to be suspicious of lovers even to the point of distrusting them indiscriminately, and so they subvert the rare reliability when they have it! These are some of the ways in which women respond to the absence of men.

Women also compensate for the absence of men. We are tempted into behaviors that help neither ourselves nor humanity. Sometimes the only help we receive from our theological tradition is the help to keep us stuck where we are. What are our compensations and temptations? What can we contribute to healthier relationships? Are there any theological escape routes out of our predicament? What can we contribute to healthier religion?

Carol Christ, at an Academy of Religion meeting, suggested that one of the theological tasks of women is to name our own particular sins. She reminded us that women have been concentrating on male sins, particularly the sins of pride and power. In a legitimate effort to distance ourselves from men's experience of sin, women have documented how it is that men use pride and power. We have also concentrated on women's gifts and strengths.

All this was necessary and understandable in the origins and early days of the women's movement. One of those origins of the women's movement in religion was a 1960 article by Valerie Saiving. That article grew in influence and became one of those quiet revolutions in thought.

Saiving was the first contemporary to identify pride and power as male sins (Valerie Saiving Goldstein, "The Human Situation"). She accomplished that by evaluating Reinhold Niebuhr's theology in the light of women's experience. She noted, for example, that excesses of power might very well be a temptation to sin for those who already had power, or access to power. Women had neither. *Too* much power therefore could hardly be women's sin. Women's sin would be quite the opposite: powerlessness. Furthermore, that pride which lusts for power could scarcely be named a woman's sin. Quite the opposite self-image and behavior was documentable among women. Women had too *little* pride, too *little* sense of self and self-worth. Feminists continue to build on Saiving's insights. Most now affirm pride and power as male temptations and female goals. Most encourage women to become less self-sacrificing and more self-loving. A generation after Saiving's dramatic alert to women, Judith Plaskow examined the theologies of Reinhold Niebuhr in much more detail, and the theology of Paul Tillich as well. Plaskow's *Sex, Sin, and Grace* is almost entirely an analysis of these men's work. Consequently, there are many examples of how men's sins endanger women and of what women's sins are not. There are, predictably, few clues about what women's sins are. The strongest and most central affirmation of women's special sin seems to be "the failure to turn toward the self."

Self-denial

Plaskow continues the description: Instead of turning to the self, women have cooperated with social structures that oppress women and encourage self-denial. It is self-denial that needs to be renounced. What needs to be claimed is self-affirmation. The "I" can reemerge within a community of women. That emergence of the self is an experience of grace.

We need to be clear that turning toward the self has nothing to do with selfishness or generosity. We are just self-less without a self. There is something missing in our separate identity. Once we get hold of a self, we may then decide to be selfish or generous. Self-lessness is the void in which those decisions do not have to be confronted. Plaskow continues the tradition of identifying women's sin as too little pride, too little sense of self. Her description of the social dimension to the tradition is particularly helpful. Sin originates in society, not in the individual. Sin is blatant in those hateful social structures that oppress. Since women's sin of co-mission is to cooperate with those structures, women's sin of omission, by implication, is not to engage in changing social structures. Women's vocation is to change the sinful social structures that oppress. In addition to the sin of too little "I" or too little pride, then, Plaskow names the women's sin of participating in our own oppression either by outright cooperation with political systems or by neglecting to change them.

I believe this tradition. I believe women must renounce self-denial, seek a self, and change whoever and whatever oppresses. I believe we need to make dramatic personal and political changes.

I also believe we need to be much more explicit and concrete about the particulars of our temptations. What are the specific ways in which we cooperate with those sinful structures? What are the particulars of women's behaviors? If we do not come clean about this, we risk the danger of failure to take responsibility for ourselves. It could be too easy to locate all the responsibility "out there" in those systems. And *who* manages those systems? Men. We can blame it all on "those men out there." When we do that, we become passive victims rather than moral agents. And woman as passive victim is no change from the old ways. A victim is just one specific form of self-denial. A victim does not assert herself or become an "I." A victim is still dependent upon someone else's definition, activities, and powers.

"Playing victim" is itself a temptation. That temptation has been realized in disquieting amounts in my experience. Insightfulness is sometimes the first step in ending the victim game. Insights can reduce a fearful history to size and perspective. Insights are just as clearly substitutes for ending the game. "I'm afraid to go downtown by myself because my father frightened me about downtown when I was ten." The question remains: Now that you're grown, are you going downtown or not? Some of us know exactly how we come to do things or don't do them, but we conveniently confuse the how of the past with decisions for the future. It's a way of keeping the victim game going.

The Inexhaustible Earth Mother

The most frequent temptation for women to compensate for our situation is to be both mother and father in the form of the Inexhaustible Earth Mother, who can be counted on to provide the breast, the lullaby, economic security, and anything else needed. It is a temptation to tolerate the irresponsibility of others. It is a temptation to let men off the hook. It is a temptation to presume enormous responsibility for the world. Insofar as we take that responsibility onto ourselves, we have our own female version of the sin of pride. We act as if we are incomparable and infinite. There are no limits to our amazing singular capacity to parent the next generation, and our own generation as well, and, of course, the old folks too. When there is trouble in a family, the woman is likely to say, "What have I done wrong?" The question not only presumes too much for herself, the question insults the other members of the family, who are relegated to a position of dimwittedness at best.

Our language is a clue to our pride as Inexhaustible Earth Mother. One of our phrases is, "It has to be done," or "Somebody has to do it." Often, what has to be done is trivial. It could be postponed or ignored altogether. Women can be distracted by petty tasks. And if somebody really has to do it, there is no reason to equate that somebody with women—unless we really believe we are the only humans who are *somebodies*.

The Illusion of Omnipotence

One of the laughs I have on myself is about woodwork and babies. I used to wash the woodwork four times a year. ("Somebody had to do it.") I began one of those washes eight months pregnant and then dutifully reported the ensuing stomach cramps to the doctor as the flu. (And that was with my second one!) Those were the Inexhaustible Earth Woman days, living in an illusion of omnipotence.

This illusion of omnipotence is not confined to the household. One of the big lies about managing in the workplace is that it is terribly demanding and draining. The reality is that much of it isn't even necessary. Women are tempted to do whatever has to be done in the workplace too. One specific temptation is to "mother" people at work by mediating disputes and calming the clients. Some women who have learned to refuse to make coffee will *not* refuse other mothering tasks. We will take inordinate responsibility unto ourselves for the lives of co-workers and customers, adding on more expended time and energy.

Then there is the clue of the exhausted look: careless dress, dark eyes. . . . Some women have a perverse pride in perpetual weariness. There is workaholism. Some workaholics repeatedly tell you about their work load past and present. They describe in detail how their tasks are impossible. They cannot be done. Of course, when they do get done, the workaholics "suffer" in relative silence, manipulating others into noticing their "virtue." It is workaholism elevated to a status of the eternal. For the Inexhaustible Earth Mother is an eternal symbol. An esteem for nature and the use of nature symbols is not a helpful way of reminding us of our constraints. Mother Nature is too powerful and eternal. The symbol reminds all too well that women are both limited to things natural and at the same time have unlimited resources as creatures of nature.

Martyrdom

Sometimes the Inexhaustible Earth Mother is a self-defined martyr. Unlike many unself-conscious mothers, she knows her behavior isn't "right." Instead of changing her behavior, however, she enjoys her suffering and sees to it that others do too. This is one of the ways to get attention and to punish simultaneously. One of the most common forms of martyrdom in the past has been this: "I gave up everything for him. I could have been—"

There is much truth in the first sentence. Women have, historically, displaced their dreams and ambitions. It's the second sentence that troubles me. One has *no way* of knowing what might have been. Furthermore, when some women have the opportunity to return to their own dreams and ambitions, they make excuses. In other words, there are occasions when martyrdom is a chosen vocation and an opportunity for refusing to take responsibility for oneself.

Since the advent of the second wave of the women's movement, there is a more insidious twist to the martyrdom tradition. Women have a conflicting set of injunctions and expectations from the women's movement. We are to follow our own dreams and become the men we wanted to marry. What does this mean for the unattached career woman who may experience being left out or left behind in the world of love dreams? And what does this mean for the middle-aged housewife with no work history or for the underemployed female? Both may experience being left out or left behind in the world of work dreams.

One of the solutions or responses to this experience goes like this: The unattached career woman is told she has love from friends and colleagues. The unemployed or underemployed woman is told she has career success in some special ways. For example, the housewife is affirmed as skillful in several areas, especially as a competent manager. Now all this is true, but there are many women for whom none of this is a choice. Their life situation does not represent the accomplishment of their dreams or even, necessarily, a part of the journey. The temptation here is to baptize one's experience as fulfillment or success. It is difficult to keep the vision on choosing our successes rather than naming anything we do as success.

The Inexhaustible Earth Mother is a female version of the male sin of pride, and we need our own version of humility in the face of it. Women need a humility that acknowledges our limits as well as worth. Curiously, limits and worth go together. Self-esteem will help us say no to others so that we can say yes to ourselves. We acknowledge finite time and energy. We acknowledge that we are human, after all. Similarly, a sense of our own worth is a realistic assessment of strengths and skills. There are limits to what we do well. We do not need the false humility that says, "Oh, it is nothing." True humility is affirming of who we are and what we can do. It is set inside the context of our humanity. There are appropriate limits for people. We are not nature. We are not God.

There are two particularly virulent expressions of the

Inexhaustible Earth Mother. The first is in the rescue of men. The second is in the rescue of children.

Rescuing Men

One of the more obvious ways to represent the Inexhaustible Earth Mother is to rescue men. We make excuses for them. We do not insist they pull their weight. We interpret, or compensate, for the failure of fathers to father. We even justify bestiality to the children: "Daddy can't help the way he is because" (pick one):

His temper takes over sometimes.

It's the liquor.

He's worried about————.

It's the way he was brought up.

He's sick.

All of the above.

Other.

I am constantly amazed at the sheer amount and variety of the punishments women absorb. Sometimes the excuses and justifications are accompanied by declarations of love as well. It's as if how much we can take is a measure of the capacity for caring.

One of the most provocative suggestions I have seen of insisting that fathers father was made by the poet Robert Bly. He suggested a one-way ticket for pubescent boys to their fathers. There are plenty of problems with the suggestion. Nevertheless, I wonder if one of the reasons single mothers have not purchased more one-way tickets is our self-image as inexhaustible and an image of fathers as incompetent. Whatever the complex motivations and situations, women are tempted to compensate for an absent father by providing endless resources to the children.

Furthermore, we make change difficult by confusing excuses with understanding. We claim there is an "understanding trap" and criticize ourselves for being too "understanding." What we mean most of the time is we are too benign. We tolerate too much. We listen too much. We pretend too much. We protect too much. We ignore too much. We complain too much. We excuse too much. I doubt that we can understand too much. Understanding and exposing our behavior make that behavior less inexorable. Understanding just might help us with the perceptions that make real changes possible and timely. Of course we cannot force or control another's behavior. We do not need to take on *ourselves*, however, somebody else's responsibility and all of the praise and guilt—mostly guilt—thereof.

Disengaging from taking responsibility is a very tricky task for women. On the one hand we say no to caretaking. On the other hand, we know that people in relationships need to tell each other what they want. There is a proper teaching function between intimates, so they will not try to be mind readers. How to teach and still not become responsible for someone else is difficult for women who have been socialized as caretakers.

Rescuing Children

As the Inexhaustible Earth Mother, we also rescue children. We expect too little and protect too much. We are tempted to become Super Mom. Sometimes that is connected to the compensation for the failure of fathers to father. Sometimes we just repeat what we learned at our own mother's knee. Sometimes the culture holds us singularly accountable and we believe it. Whatever the particular motivation or situation, Super Mom robs children of opportunities for growth and experience in the world. She hovers and smothers. She can protect the young from anything and anyone—except herself. She believes that her children belong to her like a never-born babe or a piece of property—an investment. Most of all, children receive the message that they are not responsible for themselves; someone else is their caretaker. In short, we disable children. We contribute directly to the unhealthy relationship between the sexes of the next generation by teaching them that women are the responsible ones. We teach that neither men nor women are responsible *for themselves.* That teaching not only disables personal relationships, it disables public relationships as well. That teaching gives aid and comfort to patriarchal institutions, since external authorities are reputable in public when someone else is in charge at home.

Between the absent fathers and the super mothers, it's a wonder there are as many adults as there are. It is ironic that women are tempted to take so much responsibility for the world and so little for ourselves. Insofar as we are tempted to refuse responsibility for self, we are tempted to refuse to exercise the freedom of self-transcendence in at least three ways: (1) repeating uncritically our inherited wisdoms ("We've always done it that way"), (2) maximizing our status as victims ("That's just the way it is"), or (3) permitting our legitimate anxieties about the world to close us off from the world ("I can't do anything about it").

The Abuse of Power

When we refuse to exercise the freedom of self-transcendence, we give our power away and keep too little power for ourselves. "Wait till Dad gets home" is, in fact, an extension of women's waiting, like threatening mannequins, for someone else to exercise power. For we abdicated ours. We are accustomed to think of power as securing a certain place or title in a hierarchical organization. Consequently, when a woman becomes a Director or a President, we say that she has power.

Influence

The classic definition of power for middle-class women, however, has been the power of influence. We have had access primarily as wives and secretaries to men who have titles. We have also had the power of influence with children. Our influence with children has been greatly exaggerated. Nevertheless, it is real and significant. One of the methods of using the traditional power of influence is manipulation: How can I get others to do something I want and make them believe they wanted to do it all along? One of the typical forms of manipulation in the workplace is to plant an idea with one of those titled men and help him believe it was his own. Sometimes this is intentional, because we have learned that a titled man's ideas have a better chance of implementation. One of the helpful struggles within the women's movement is to identify a broad range of different kinds of power and different styles of using that power. Furthermore, there is a helpful vision of creating organizations and decisions where power is shared. Women are more likely to view power as infinite, limitless. Therefore, in order for me to have more power, I do not need for someone else to have less. There's plenty to go around. In fact, the appropriate use of my power could actually help others use their power rather than diminish it. This vision is connected with the critique of manipulation. Manipulation is no longer reputable. Manipulation tends to be viewed now as a sneaky and cowardly style of a second-rate power—the power of influence. Women increasingly want, in short, an up-front power that can empower others, and we want it in a style of collegial and mutual decision-making.

Some temptations have intruded into this vision, which, ironically, have resulted in new forms of giving away our power and new forms for using traditional patriarchal power.

Power as Evil

One of those temptations is to denounce power as evil. Sometimes all forms of power are denounced as evil, which excuses women from participating in it at all. I see no substantive difference between this posture and the socialized habits of women which have kept us from participation in the world of decision-making outside the home. Perhaps the only difference is expectation. Now that we know the world just might be open to us, we feel a greater need to justify our unwillingness to live there. Defining power as evil is the excuse to abdicate responsibility for the outcome of those worldly decisions.

Sometimes a certain kind of power is denounced as evil: the finite, unshared, controlling power of patriarchal systems. This accusation provides an excuse for refusing to take on one of those "bigger" titles or positions and an opportunity for resenting women who do. (Resenting those other women can also, of course, be just a respectable feminist cover for jealousy.) More important, denouncing that kind of power as evil provides a safe, self-righteous place from which to criticize others, even if it is from "within" a system at a modest decision-making level. There are, of course, stresses for women who hold titles in patriarchal systems, and our limited success in changing those systems and ourselves in them is not of itself sinful. What is sinful is the pretense that we do not share the responsibility for the outcome.

Not Belonging

One of the things that veil our temptations from us is the belief that we do not really belong here. This church is not our home. This world is not our home. Surely this system is not our home. At one level this is good theology, for what we now experience is neither normative nor ultimate. At another level, this is a description of woman's reality; most of our realities have been defined and organized by men. At still another level, however, not belonging is just a cop-out. If I don't really belong, I don't really have responsibility for what happens.

There are certain advantages to a sense of not belonging. Allegiances are clearer and risk-taking is easier. There has not been enough concentration on the *dis*advantages. The disadvantage to not belonging is irresponsibility, which invites sins of separation, alienation, and self-righteousness. It is a way of giving away our power by blaming and therefore confirming the power of men. This is one of the situations in which the symbol of God as Mother nurtures us and holds us accountable. A Mother God symbol calls us both into belonging and into taking the responsibility that goes with it.

One of the most clear situations in which to gain insight about our own temptations to abuse power is in groups comprised of all women or nearly all women. Here is an opportunity to act out some of the vision of shared power and collective, open decision-making. Those things do happen. I have experienced healthy consensus as a way of making decisions. I have experienced the tolerance for groups to arrive at multiple decisions. By stark contrast, I have also experienced consensus as a cover-up for manipulation, while refusing to act is blamed on the men who are not even in the room. When no vote is taken and no clear alternative method for consensus exists, whoever declares a consensus casts a single ballot for what she wants. Many groups will allow that bullet vote to stand rather than insist on a head count. Having been outvoted so often, women can be overly solicitous of a minority opinion, even to the point of disenfranchising themselves anew. During the experiments with decision-making methods designed to include the minority, women's groups are vulnerable to the tyranny of that minority. The greatest temptation in women's groups in the absence of a clear decision-making alternative is to fall back on the experience of manipulation. The temptation in women's groups in the absence of men is to blame them for our immobilization. In either case, we give away our up-front power. That giveaway, and the irresponsibility that goes with it, is a formidable temptation to abuse power.

Abandonment

Another abuse of power is our abandonment of men. We exaggerate their awesomeness by separation and so step out of touch with reality. Like the exaggerated influence of the absent father on the children, exiled men have a disproportionate influence on women. Distanced people are unknown people, objects of speculation and stereotyping. At a distance, men can easily resemble an army. Up close, they are just wearing fatigues. Further, there is the abandonment of children to the abusive extremes of patriarchal power. Some women will not only tolerate but support the bestiality of fathers to children, while others excuse those who do and so become collaborators in bestiality. Still others collaborate by pretending ignorance. Pretending: Women are tempted by the conspiracy of silence about fathers. We are tempted to hide some things from our children and ignore some other things. There are times when we must do that. There are times when we make mistakes in judgments about which things to reveal and which to conceal. That is scarcely a cause for accusations. What is accusatory is hiding from the children to protect *ourselves* and pretending it's for their good. Hiding the father or the father's whereabouts is a common error. Another is to stay with the father and pretend it is "for the children's sake."

Playing God

Women as well as men play God. Woman as the Inexhaustible Earth Mother comes very close to playing God.

Sometimes we cross the boundary and wholeheartedly act out God's part. We forget our finitude and neglect our humanity. There is an arena in which we are even more centered on the activity of God. That arena is love. Women are tempted to usurp God's infinite capacity for unconditional love. Men may grasp at power of the Almighty. Women long for the love of the Almerciful.

This sin is encouraged by the church. Recall the preaching you have heard on the subject of love. One of the themes or slogans in those sermons is: "People who want to be loved should find someone *else* to love." There are two unstated expectations in that slogan. The first is that if you find others to love, they will love you back; the other is that you already have received enough love, so you can literally afford the grace to give some away and that will make you feel better; either way, there's something in it for you.

This is a man's sermon. It is a sermon thoroughly informed by male experience. For boys and men in our culture are the ones who are most likely to receive love and nurture from mothers and lovers. So they have the surplus and therefore can with grace give some away. It may be that the preacher has (consciously or subconsciously) the women parishioners in mind as the primary hearers of that sermon. Sensitive clergymen may very well sense women's gaping needs. They are truly bewildered by those needs. The "find somebody to love" sermon could be an honest response to that awareness in *women* from *his* experience.

His bewilderment and her gaping needs are set into the context of the reliable mother, which is not only the empirical reality but the cultural ideal against which women are measured and judged. Women try to measure up against this cultural ideal with our reliability. In doing so, we are tempted to love so constantly and indiscriminately that we are God-like in our endless capacity, patience, and long-suffering. We are even tempted to imitate God's redemptive love both as mothers and as lovers. We are sure we can save others from this or that, especially the children.

In the process of loving the children, mothers absorb punishment from children. Some of that is a part of the job description. Any child needs to press against the limits and constraints of authority and another self. One of the child's first words is "no." Another is "I" (more likely "me"). An important early sentence is "No, I will." No to parent; yes to the self. Resistance is acted out even more forcefully. Rage accompanies limits. Words and actions that worry and weary a mother are inevitable and proper. Most mothers know this is part of the child's development. A mother's struggle is to support a child's growing away in some context of safety and acceptance and still maintain her sanity. In that struggle and in that sense, a mother loves unconditionally. She does not withhold support and affection even when the child is the most troublesome. The child may receive a quality of love in the midst of trouble that no one else would consider. She will be there, no matter what.

When the little boy grows up and marries a woman, what has he learned about the quality of a woman's love? He has learned that if she loves him she will be there, *no matter what.* If she is intolerant or, worse, leaves him, he feels rejected, abandoned, and unloved. Because a mother would "love you just the way you are."

When the little girl grows up, what has she learned about the quality of love? She has learned that unconditional love comes from woman, who she now is. She expects to give it to a man. She does not expect to receive it from a man. Or, if she generalizes from the reliable mother, she does expect to receive it from a man and she has a good chance of being disappointed. In any case, she expects to give love in a way that approaches the love of God. Just plain Bill. He's not much, but *I love him still.* (*Why?*) The experience and training of love is still that different between the sexes. Telling women who need love to give love is to condemn us to the classical function of Gods and idealized mothers. Why? Partly because the church confirms our childhood training. God so loved (her) that she also ought to love others. *In the same way that God loved. In the same way that mother is supposed to love.*

Under the conditions of reliable and idealized mothers, women are endangered by a theology of God's gracious love. Because the connection is made between that love of God "in heaven" and women's love "on earth." So it is that both women and men expect that women will love unconditionally. By contrast, both women and men expect that women will earn love, that there is something conditional about it. All this makes women responsible not only for the relationship but also for male behavior. That is an overwhelmingly female script. Obligations for behavior rest so lopsidedly on women that many men will presume no possibility of change: "Hey, baby, that's the way I am." Still others will "test" her love with the capacity to "put up with." How much will she ignore or tolerate? Will she be there no matter what, just like Mom? We know that most batterers are genuinely surprised when a woman fights back or leaves. A batterer feels unjustly deserted by her acts of self-defense. He feels persecuted, assaulted, and fights back. He is living out of a child's expectation of its mother's love. That expectation is unwittingly reinforced by a doctrine of God's love, which is free, patient, long-suffering, merciful, and redemptive. Consequently, one of the male sayings in one form or another goes like this: "What's *your* problem with *my* behavior?" Which means, *You* have an obligation to justify or explain yourself as to what *I've* done. And that's crazy. And the even crazier thing is *we do just that.* This is one of our most concrete behaviors inside the big temptation to sin by playing God or, rather, by playing Mother Goddess and Idealized Mother.

I was past forty before I realized that these male sayings were not just cop-outs and excuses for what they knew perfectly well to be improper. Most men are not kidding. They are telling the truth. They really have a set of expectations and are genuinely bewildered with women's resentment over trying to meet them. They are genuinely surprised when we refuse. Many men say, "I don't beat and I don't cheat. Why is she mad at me?" They are truly surprised that their *not* doing some things is inadequate. I'll never forget the man who called me to tell me that his wife was gone. His only commentary was, "I didn't even know she was mad at me." I knew. I knew for as long as I knew her. Here are two sentences that describe the small, significant difference in the expectations of men and women. She says, "He doesn't love me because he's not here, so I'm leaving." He says, "She's leaving me because I'm not here, so she doesn't love me." Both have loved each other out of expectations formed in the context of the reliable mothers and a theology of the enormity of gracious love and grace. That is also why the curse "motherf——," the ultimate curse that men hurl at each other, is so traumatic. That curse is traumatic because it is too close to the truth. To become a mother lover is precisely the expectation and goal for men in our culture.

Women cooperate with these sinful arrangements by trying to act out with some enthusiasm and arrogance the gracious love of God. We give until we are depleted and then punish ourselves with guilt for being empty. In this form of playing Mother Goddess, we deny our finitude and refuse to deal with our humanity. In trying to hoard the vastness of loving, we claim the accompanying qualities of sacrifice, patience, care, support, and suffering as peculiarly ours. In this process, we become puffed up with our own version of power: the power to keep children and men infantile. We deny the full humanity of children and men by cutting them off from their own growth and potential. And to make matters worse, we accuse someone else out there of being responsible for the whole situation even as we continue the task of primary parent who instructs and

models. There are feminist theologians who make the
explicit connection between the Mother God and mothers
as both representing unconditional love. That is a very
precarious and dangerous connection to make in this
historical context of the reliable and idealized mother
experience. An earthly love between partners requires
exchanges and negotiations. There are legitimate demands
on children as well as lovers. It may help us to remember
that Jesus has conditions: "You are my friends *if* . . . "
God's love is set alongside judgment and justice. In other
words, God's love is also demanding. God's people are
accountable for what they do. But we are having enough
trouble playing God. I suspect that in this situation the
language of unconditional love needs to be abandoned
altogether. We need to disconnect the images of Idealized Mother and Mother Goddess from that kind of love so
as to discourage women from abusive behavior against
ourselves and others by presuming *our* infinity and *their*
infantilism.

Furthermore, in the human situation, that all-
encompassing love is too connected with the real-life ordinary mother. She is the one who is counted on for
perpetual presence. She dispenses acceptance and forgiveness. Forgiveness for what? Forgiveness for acts, yes. In
classical reformed theology we are also forgiven for who
we are as well as what we do. Specifically, we are forgiven
for our self-interest. Self-interest is essential to our survival
as humans and has become man's special prerogative. It's a
little crazy to be forgiven for being human, for not being
God. Why should I be forgiven for that? I wasn't born God,
and I am admonished not to take God's place. Mothers
don't forgive who the children are. In fact, mothers are
more likely to believe that the children are wonderful—
usually out of proportion to reality. Mothers are more
likely to forgive what children do. In that sense, mothers
are smarter than a classical description of God. Mothers

know that we do not need some ontological excuse for being human.

In short, we need to detach that imbalanced, powerful image of God's love from mother love and detach forgiveness from being human. In human affairs the mother has become too much the institutionalized mirror of the reliable love of God. At the same time, she has become the sought-after lover of the adult male who learned the content of love in Christian categories at his mother's knee. That is not a saving story for women. It is a losing story for women in this historical situation.

On the other hand, a loving, accepting God who expects both men and women to survive as humans, who forgives what we do, and who journeys with us can provide the context for change. I am struck by the capacity for church folk to grow and change when we begin with the facts of God's love and acceptance and the love and acceptance of the community. We can literally afford to change because we are not under assault and have no need to defend ourselves. The heavy repetition of judgments, admonitions, and challenges doesn't do it, because guilt is the only certain outcome. One of the reasons liberal causes burn out is that guilt consumes the fire. The accused repentant white man will take on cumulative historical guilt and either be overwhelmed and immobilized by it or will engage in frantic activity for the purpose of expiation, which cannot last. For justice to hold up over the long haul, that man doesn't have to like me but he does have to like himself. His theological tradition, which tends to spank him for his self-centeredness, his pride, might make him feel bad from time to time. But there is no motivation in that for him to change his behavior. In fact, his sorrow can easily become a substitute for change. Insofar as that substitute is operative, the long-suffering, patient, gracious unconditional love of God and mother is not a saving story for him either.

Not Telling the Truth

Finally, we do not tell the truth. We do not trust what we see. Even when we are sure that the emperor is naked, we do not mention the fact. Women lie by ignoring, mistrusting, or misrepresenting our own experience. This is one of the ways in which we abdicate responsibility. Cowardice feeds deceit.

First, we want so much to please others that we lack the courage to face the truth and name it. Sometimes we avoid the truth out of the bizarre belief that we may yet receive affection by giving, even though millions of women's lives show otherwise. Thus, our capacity for deceit multiplies. Sometimes we try to please out of our Mother Goddess complex. Sometimes pleasing is an uncritical habit. By whatever route we arrive at the need to please, we tend to please too many without enough discrimination of who we are pleasing and why. A behavior that accompanies pleasing is indecisiveness. Many women are reluctant or unwilling to make hard decisions. We also postpone decisions. Sometimes, of course, postponing a decision is a helpful decision in itself and needs more of a place of honor in decision-making. At the same time, women frequently just duck decisions. We know that women are more likely to ask questions and men are more likely to give answers. Women need to participate in the answers. When women participate in the answers, we still do so often by indirect means. We hint. "Maybe that's not all there is to it" (O.K., so what else is there to it?). We use body language instead of a no vote. Hand-wringing and tears can register displeasure while refusing to take responsibility for the outcome. We substitute complex diversionary analysis instead of saying straight out what we want. Finally, there is the screaming silence that holds all in contempt along the decision-making way. One of the ingredients in these behaviors is the unwillingness to make decisions and take responsibility for them. One of the implications of refusing decision-making is to leave those decisions in the hands of people who may not share the experiences and insights of women that need to go into those decisions. Pleasing too much can lead us to eschew the power by which our moral contributions can be activated. The desire to please others is one of the ingredients that helps us keep up the lie. We hide in front of our experience.

A second reason for not telling the truth is fear. We are afraid of rejection, punishment, uncertainties, humiliation. We are afraid of our own individuality as real separated selves who may name their own realities as inherently and automatically valid. Even when we do identify our separate experience, many women still use it as a reference to male experience: The male experience is seen as the truly valid one; ours is deviant. Our need to please and our fear of not pleasing masks the realities of our own experience, which we refuse to uncover. We choose instead to identify or compare with the male experience. In the same day, two different women in two different conversations asked me if I trusted my memory. We had shared similar childhood experiences. Each remembered that the adults in their lives contradicted that experience, saying, No, it didn't happen that way. Children cannot take the responsibility for that contradiction and the ensuing confusion.

Children are much more dependent upon others for a reality check than adults. When we are grown, however, there is the temptation still to hang on to those adults' interpretations; there is the temptation to continue to let others name our experience. This is of no value to anybody. What we are communicating to other people in our lives is that they are not important enough to hear the truth. We are telling them that they are not worth having a real self as a partner and friend.

Some women will say in response that they have tried to communicate their real self and are not heard. They have therefore given up, because it doesn't seem to make any difference. What this usually means is that *he* doesn't change in the way *she* wants him to change. That is a trap and a link back to our efforts to manipulate or manage someone else. The point of communicating who we are and sharing our experience is not to change someone else. It is to change us. We are not responsible for the ways in which other people respond to that change in us. It is practice in letting go of the consequences.

Peggy Way has a wonderful sermon on the rich young ruler that demonstrates that model of letting go. She does not concentrate on the rich young ruler who went away sorrowfully because Jesus told him to relinquish his riches. She concentrates on Jesus' model for ministry, which is summarized dramatically in the last sentence of the sermon: "And Jesus did not go running after him." He shared himself and let go of the consequences.

That brings us back full circle to women's first sin: the sin of self-denial. Women need repentance. We need to strengthen the struggle to become selves. We need to fill ourselves up with conditional love of ourselves and others. This love is not only for our sakes. It is for humanity's sake. Humanity does not need lying, hiding, false-naming, emptying, abusing power, and rescuing. Humanity does need a kind of love to cast out fears for the future. That kind of love requires becoming selves with others.

> For squandering our energy
> and hating our power,
>
> Mother, forgive us.
>
> For worshiping a false father
> **And** hating ourselves,
>
> Father, forgive us.
>
> For pretending that we know not
> What we see and do,
>
> God, have mercy.

4

Experience
and the Bible

Women's temptations and compensations are related in part to our vision of who God is as Parent. The dangers are particularly present in two situations. One is when we identify with God as Mother, who is distorted as the gracious, patient, merciful long-suffering, inexhaustible source of love and care. In this situation we are tempted to imitate her. The idealized mother of our social environment encourages that imitation. The second situation is when we disengage from God as Father, who is distorted as the patriarchal stereotype invested with self-hating characteristics. The patriarchal images of masculinity in our social environment encourage that disengagement.

Against these powerful images and traditions we need to look for alternative images of both female and male and especially of mothers and fathers. We need to do this so that both women and men will grow into the fullness of our humanity and be accountable as responsible moral agents. There are at least three resources to help us give fresh content to the parenting symbols and move us along the human quest: the experience of absence, people and language, and the Bible.

The Experience of Absence

First of all, the experience of absence is in itself a resource. Russians write about freedom, warriors dream of peace, slaves sing of liberty, men imagine birthing: What they all know is what is absent. They face the emptiness and create out of it. The creative act is God-like activity. Like God, we look directly into the void, the emptiness. The creative act begins with a blank piece of paper or a blank canvas. It begins in silence.

Creativity begins with cultural emptiness, also. It is noticing that an institution is empty and pointless. Creativity requires that we not only *notice* that the emperor has no clothes but have the courage to say he is naked. In one sense the Christian faith begins with the empty tomb. There is confession of the emptiness and grief over the loss. That emptiness and grief are part of the content of death before resurrection. But resurrection does require death. Creativity requires confession of the emptiness. The creative act is risky, to be sure, and it requires enormous tenacity to stick with the creation. The temptation is to fall back on the familiarity of alienating symbols. But it is one of the ways into new content for parenting symbols.

People and Language

Second, just folks. The fathering man is a resource. He is a living model of how a fathering man looks and feels and acts. He is also a formidable reminder that the intimacies of parenting are not the exclusive characteristics of mothers. There is a strong bias in our culture to identify any nurturing parental activity as female. The common use of the words "mother" and "mothering" reveals this bias. For example, fathers who go to prepare food and feed children will often say, "I'm the mother today." Men who give comforting hugs often refer to that as "mothering." The nurturing functions are so strongly associated with mothers that fathers who do them are identified as mothers. They are not mothers. They are fathers. The worldly woman is a resource. She is a living model of how an active woman looks and feels and acts. She is a formidable reminder that activities in worldly affairs are not the exclusive characteristic of fathers. The common usage for her activity has been masculine. Golda Meier was once called the only man in the Israeli cabinet. She was not a man. She was a woman and a mother.

The history of the psychoanalytic movement encourages us to keep the qualities of the sexes different and separate from each other. Freud did acknowledge in a 1925 article that "masculine" and "feminine" may be theoretical constructs inherent in both biological men and women. But he did not pursue the idea and fell back on investing the sexes with utterly different characteristics. Men, for him, were aggressive and sought to displace their fathers. Men were nearly patriarchal stereotypes. God as Father was set up as the super-masculine patriarch so that human sons really had little choice but to rebel or obey, in a structured inalienation. Jung did pick up on "masculine" and "feminine" as theoretical constructs. He called these characteristics "archetypes" and located these archetypes inside both biological sexes. Theoretically, this could have helped us with a more fluid view of men and women. I think it has not helped. True, both sets of characteristics in this model are available to both sexes. That is surely an improvement. At the same time, it gives permission to both sexes to stay separated from real-life members of the other sex and encourages alienation both from each other and from oneself. If women have male characteristics inside themselves, there is no need to engage men. If men have female characteristics inside themselves, there is no need to engage women. More importantly, in this model, the mother must borrow the skills of logic from masculine sources. The virtues of that image are not her own. She will have to refer to that competency as masculine and be alienated from both masculinity and herself as female. The father must borrow the intimacies of parenting from feminine sources. The virtues of that image are not his own. He will have to refer to that nurturing as mothering and be alienated from both femininity and himself as male. Jungian language and symbols have a popularity right now among feminists, who display these symbols as affirming female characteristics. I agree that nurturing characteristics need to be affirmed. I do not agree that nurturing should be labeled feminine. "Feminine" labels cannot possibly be disassociated from women, and the fact that we women are the nurturers is a statement of the problem, not a solution.

Another kind of affirmation comes from Carol Gilligan. Gilligan has helped all of us by research that is based on women's experience. Her work helps us to remember that psychoanalysis was based on men's experience, which then became normative for humanity. By describing women's moral decision-making as distinctive, she has helped end the view of men's decision-making as normative. That description of women's moral decision-making can be summarized as women's preference for a self-in-relationships as compared with men's preference for a self-in-separation. When I hear women use her data as evidence for women's moral superiority, I have the same *click!* feeling as I do when men are named morally superior. I should like for us not to replicate the man's error and presume that whatever we do is better. There are some practical situations in which independent and autonomous behavior is necessary. First, we cannot always make decisions that are the least harmful to everybody concerned. After all the data are in and everyone is heard and all the options laid out, there will still be confrontations, and hurting decisions will be made by somebody. Women need to claim a self-in-separation just as men need to claim more of a self-in-relationship.

Images of parents each of whom share both virtues is a resource to human parents, who can more fully express them as godlike, Godly. We need to turn to the real-life fathering man and name that fathering. We need intentionally to use the name of father as an image of reliability and care. We increasingly do use images of public strength for mother and thereby help her into existence—and into politics, science, and business. We can also increasingly use the nurturing strength of father and call him into existence. We need to end these alienating "masculine only" images of God the Father and "feminine only" images of God the Mother. We can use gentleness as associated with both male and female and strength for both male and female. In short, real-life women and men who confound stereotypes are resources to parenting symbols. Conversely, a use of parenting language that confounds stereotypes can help bring into reality more of these real-life women and men.

The Bible

Third, the Bible is a resource. Granted, the Bible also describes patriarchy for both people and God; it is not a single-minded model for all our images and behaviors. The Bible does have within it, however, images, stories, models, and language which count against patriarchy. The Bible is a better resource than we have been led to believe by subsequent patriarchal religion. The Bible is a better resource than is claimed by many feminists. This does not mean that women's humanity and liberation stand or fall on the weight of the Bible. We do not need to wait for the latest round of biblical information and insight to tell us who we are and what we are worth. The Bible does have other kinds of authority, not the least of which is its great influence on the culture. It is in the air we breathe and the quick ethical decisions we make. For this reason it is a powerful resource to feminists and is rejected or neglected at great cost.

The Bible is a resource on parenting symbols in two dramatic ways. First, the Bible has a rich range of meaning in female symbols. One of the symbols is mother, which on the one hand explicitly connects biological parenting with

God and on the other hand enlarges the symbol of mother beyond biological parenting. Second, the Bible has male symbols for God that are larger than patriarchal symbols of domination and violence. One of those symbols is God as Father, which stands over against patriarchy. Furthermore, Jesus' Father represents a critique of the patriarchal family.

Female Symbols: God as Mother

The Scripture does have a variety of female symbols and stories that are increasingly discovered and used in the churches. Sometimes those images are explicitly maternal. For example, in Numbers 11, Moses' complaint to God projects onto God the images of birthing and wet-nursing. Moses does not want the level of responsibility that comes with parenting, which he believes is God's responsibility as the One who created as both Mother and Father. Hosea has maternal images for God, again alongside of paternal images, through the feeding and teaching tasks that were then associated with mothers. Isaiah 42:14 and Deuteronomy 32:18 also illustrate God as Mother. In Isaiah, the image is of a woman in labor. In Deuteronomy, the image is coupled with the Father image. The subject is a common theme: the turning away from Yahweh and the turning to other gods. A part of the lament says, "You forgot the God who gave you birth." Isaiah 66:9–13 describes Yahweh as birthing with an open womb and then nursing and comforting on the breast. Psalm 131:2 also uses the breast image. The psalmist is calmed "like a child quieted at its mother's breast." Both passages describe Yahweh as providing uniquely mother comfort. The good news in explicit biological mothering symbols is that these biblical resources contradict patriarchy's debasing of biological mothering into female carnality.

Sometimes the tradition has obscured the explicitly maternal, just as the patriarchal tradition has repressed many things feminine. For example, in Jeremiah 31:20, God is speaking of the favored child. For the third line, which reads that God's "heart yearns for him," Phyllis Trible's translation (which uses both an expert analysis of the language and the context of the passage) reads, "My womb trembles for him." The words "pity" and "compassion" are linguistically rooted in the word for "womb." When we read of God's "pity," there is in some sense an analogy to God as mother. When we read "pity" together with explicit father language, there is the good news that God as both Mother and Father is the compassionate Parent.

In addition to explicit mothering texts, other biblical texts have mothering components inside of larger female images. For example, we now know that the Holy Spirit is a female image in at least three ways. First, linguistically, the Hebrew for spirit of God is feminine. Second, the feminine principle of wisdom is often linked with the Spirit. Third, the spirit is used in the tradition as a female symbol. The Holy Spirit takes on an especially significant mother symbol as parent-creator of Jesus, both in his biological birthing and in his rebirthing at baptism, when he receives the gift of the Spirit. In some of the Apocryphal and Gnostic writings, the Holy Spirit is explicitly mother. The female spirit, however, represents activity that is larger than the task usually associated with mothering. It is true that the ancients present birthing, nursing, feeding, teaching, and comforting as God's mothering. It is also true that they present wisdom and a more comprehensive creativity as associated with the feminine. The connection among female, wisdom, and God is explicit in Proverbs. The Mother Wisdom God is sometimes connected in God's activity of creating (Ps. 104:24; 136:5). This presentation is a remarkable inheritance from a culture in which mother-hood was the greatest aspiration available to women. We need to reclaim the larger Mother God as part of the biblical witness. At the same time we must acknowledge that mothering does not exhaust for us the image of God—

and the image of ourselves—as feminine. We need also to reclaim the larger image of creativity and wisdom. Those characteristics do not exhaust images of the feminine, either. Still, they are resources to us. There is a passion in searching for or describing female divinity, because it is like discovering oneself; because she is like us and we are like her. We are fully human. We belong here. Relevance is a key issue. What difference does it make that a Mother God has lived? Or does live? Or can be birthed by feminist imagination?

For Judeo-Christian theologians, relevance goes beyond both the image of God and equality arguments. The image of the female God makes women fully human, which in turn promotes equality of the sexes. The presence of feminine divinity in the tradition helps legitimate that tradition as credible religion. We not only belong here in this world, we belong in these churches and in these synagogues. They are ours.

This is probably one of the reasons why the Mary myth maintained such a strong hold in the tradition. In one way or another, her earthly counterparts could see themselves as participants in spiritual life. The idea makes so much sense, in fact, it is remarkable that Protestants could suppress Mary as successfully as we did. On the other hand, that suppressed femininity turned up partly in the pastor's wife and later in women clergy. It is deliciously ironic that Mary as mother could be so repressed and still turn up again as real-life mothers in pulpits exercising authority in the name of God the Father! Once we have that authority, we also have the authority for theological disputation and subversion. Nevertheless, both Catholic and Protestant patriarchy withheld female power by suppressing female symbols. Mary's elevated position emerged because she was Somebody's mother, while Protestants elevated motherhood itself. Both mothers remained one step removed from an open, separate, independent, and authenticating image of femaleness in the world. Female images were so suppressed in the Christian tradition that they emerged only in the shadow of God as Father as one who births the Son or the church.

But suppression does not abolish the resources. One of those resources is the Mary symbol, which goes beyond mothering. She confounds the female stereotype. One of her characteristics that commends her to the religious imagination is the tough, prophetic side of her in the Magnificat, which is perceived as "masculine" by our culture and which is very much a part of this woman. Furthermore, the Magnificat (Luke 1:46–55) contains the same prophetic message that is in Jesus' first sermon. The spirit of the Lord was upon them both, and they both proclaimed good news to the poor and the outcast. Both announced a new day. Both represented the prophetic tradition.

There are other resources in the tradition that confound the stereotypical female myth. For example, in the book of Judges, Deborah led an army while Jael murdered the opposing commander. The example may not be particularly attractive, but it does confound female stereotypes. These are the behaviors usually attributed to males. There are other expanding symbols for women in the Bible. There is the heroic, invincible woman of Revelation 12, who represents Israel and perhaps Christ also as a female ingredient in the community and in God. And, to return to the mother symbol, there is Eve, the theologian, discussing the big questions with God. There is at least as much mother image of God in the parable of the lost coin as there is father image of God in the parable of the prodigal son. Fortunately, many of these stories and symbols are being recovered by feminist Christians and are now available to us.

Male Symbols: God as Father

What especially interests me in this context is the image of fathers, especially God as Father. We know there are

advantages for feminists in seeing a larger view of female
and in seeing God as Mother. What are the values in seeing
God as Father?

We have already noted in chapter 1 that the biblical God
is described as reliable. Furthermore, as a Father, that God
can be trusted to engage in the responsibilities of parenting. The Scriptures also give additional helpful content to
God as Father. It is a happy fact that the tradition helps us
in that particular way, for it is the imaging of a Father who
fathers that we need. We also conceded some unhappy
facts about the biblical God's patriarchal behavior. Let us
ask an additional question or so: To what extent are the
patriarchal behaviors of dominance and violence integral
to God's fathering? When God punishes, for example, is
God punishing in the image of a Father?

Joanna Bos has recorded the infrequent use of the
explicit word "father" for God in the Old Testament. In
five of twelve situations, the word is used in a special
context, designating a particular relationship between God
and King. In the other seven cases, the content of fathering
is recalling the children home and reconciling with them.
This language associated with fathering is clearly not the
language of transcendent dominance which we associate
with patriarchy. Rather, it is a language of care, closeness,
and compassion. In Psalm 103:13, God as Father treats the
children tenderly. This is one of those texts in which "pity"
(from "womb") is combined with explicit father language.
The father feels in the way mothers are supposed to feel.
The Mother-Father God is compassionate Parent. In
Deuteronomy 13:6, for example, the Father is the creator
of the child and the one who calls the child home. In
Jeremiah 31:9, the Father leads the firstborn back home
also. Furthermore, God comforts the child along the way,
providing a smooth path and fresh water. In Isaiah 63:16,
the Father rescues and redeems. Compassion is called
forth from the Father Redeemer. In Deuteronomy 32:13
and 18 the Father and the Mother feed and procreate. In

Hosea 11 the Father is a patient Parent who feeds and teaches. In all these cases the father image is distinguished from the images of domination and violence. There is in Hosea 11 both the use of intimate parent metaphors and the use of transcendent judgment. Yahweh is anguished by the wanderings of Israel. In one moment the jealous God is fierce. In another moment the God as Parent remembers teaching the child to walk, holding the child, and cannot give up that wandering child who is so beloved. The tenderness of the parent restrains and mediates the right-eous judgment of God. It can be argued that judgment is not an activity of fathering at all. In any case, judgment is not the primary activity in Hosea's account. The love of the suffering God is the primary activity.

Seven explicit texts do not exhaust father imagery in the Old Testament. There are additional passages that use father or mother metaphors implicitly, and many of them reinforce the tender imagery of these explicit texts. For example, one of the marks of the King as a representative of God and of God as King Creator, is as Father of the fatherless (Ps. 68:5; Deut. 10:18). Orphans are the special responsibility of the King and the special children of God.

There are two helpful implications in recalling these passages. One is that there are significant biblical resources on God as Father that image attractive fathering. Second, the images are separable from the transcendent patriarchal images of dominance and violence. Those two things can help us remember a sense of caution as we turn to the Scriptures. One is to be careful about collecting up all the ugly father images out of our human experience and depositing them onto God as Father. The second is to be careful not to accuse the biblical writers of doing that same thing. Apparently, those writers did not just project a patriarchal power onto God and name that fathering. Their sense of fathering was much better than that. Even in the larger context of God as judge as well as parent, Yahweh is viewed as a suffering God. He is the one who suffered the profound grief of parents who see wayward children en route to destruction. God kept calling to and recalling the children of Israel. There was forgiveness, reconciliation, and new beginnings. That image is still a powerful source of strengthening the father image and a challenge to human fathering.

The Father of Jesus

The tender parental symbol of God is for the first time used as a direct address by Jesus. Father God was never used as direct address in the Old Testament, nor is it known to have been a form of address in Jesus' day. By contrast, Jesus addressed God as Abba, the intimate form for father. "Abba" was an ordinary way for a child affectionately to address the father, as in "dear father." Our current use of "daddy" is a first step toward understanding the content of this close, bonding language.

Jesus always used this language, according to the gospel (for example, Rom. 8:15; Gal. 4:6), with only one exception. That exception is the cry of separation and despair from the cross: "My God, my God, why have you forsaken me?" It is significant that it is in such a situation of isolation and alienation that Jesus uses transcendent, powerful God language. It is just as significant that Jesus did not call out to a father in the moment of experiencing abandonment. God as Father does not abandon. The reliability of Yahweh as parent was surely confirmed in that choice of language.

In every other situation, Jesus uses the intimate, familial God language. By the use of this "Abba" language there is a shift toward even more emphasis on the nearness and tenderness of God as parent and less emphasis on the patriarchal motif of hierarchical domination. "Considering its initial subversiveness, it is ironic to see 'Father' pressed into the service of hierarchy," Janet Morley writes. It is indeed ironic. It is also politically naive and dangerous to the self-interest of feminism to equate or attach father symbols and patriarchy indiscriminately. Instead, here in the language of Jesus there is an implicit critique of patriarchy, albeit an ambiguous one. For one thing, the language is exclusive male language. Probably Jesus made that linkage to a Jewish family whose blood kin were collected around the household of one father. The message was that his relationship with God was *that* close. It is still exclusive language. For another thing, the language may include in some instances the *obedience* of the devoted child as well as the *affections* of the devoted child. Obedience carries with it a hierarchical model of domination. Accomplishing that domination by love rather than by brute force is a significant improvement.

Still, obedience from love does not abolish the ingredient of domination. For example, it is argued that Jesus' prayer in the Garden to the Father was a declaration of obedience: not my will, but yours. Jesus' death would be a decision for obedience to the external Father. One can also view Jesus' passion as a consequence of his ministry. Integrity and faithfulness carry risks. Further, the Father was not that clearly external, separate. Jesus' prayer was, in short, larger and more complex than a kind of leaving the decision entirely somewhere else.

Insofar as the symbols of obedience are present, however, the language has limits for feminists. Nevertheless, Jesus' use of God as Father expresses the core of his relationship to God, which is intimacy and compassion and is different from domination and violence. The Scriptures reveal a God who is larger than patriarchal models. The Scriptures also reveal a God as Father who is closer and more attractive than patriarchal models. Jesus' use of the symbol helps us come nearer to an alternative content for fathers and for fathering.

The Family

Jesus' use of the symbol also suggests an alternative definition of the family itself. Jesus not only used Father for himself, he taught the disciples to say "Father." Here, there is the strongest connection with the Old Testament theme of becoming kin to God by adoption rather than by blood ties. God adopts or elects Israel as the special child heir. God adopts also kings of Israel as special sons. When Jesus used father language, he did not refer to a relationship with humanity inclusively or with himself exclusively. Instead, he was referring to a relationship to disciples by adoption. The Gospels always show Jesus' use of Father to pertain to the disciples. (There is one exception in Matthew 23:9, and we shall return to this passage.) The early church emphasized a different kind of familial connection among the disciples who were of one father by adoption The themes of faith and grace are connected to kinship by adoption. It is the Father's activity of adoption-grace and the people's response in faith that make up this new family of God.

The theme is especially strong in Romans, Galatians, and Ephesians. In Romans 8:14–17, Paul declares the church as the children of God. The children call God "Abba," Father. For it is through the Spirit that these disciples become children of the father. In Galatians 3, Paul remembers that Abraham was a son of God because of faith. He was adopted. He then tells the Christians that they are also children of God by faith. They are adopted. Ephesians continues the promise of the family status to Gentiles, who are also heirs of the Father through faith. It is partly because of this new family arrangement that the word "children" becomes a typical name for these new Christians. Becoming a Christian was becoming a child of God by adoption. Those children composed the new household of faith. So Jesus defined family positively as discipleship. At the same time, that definition of family was set over against the biological and patriarchal family.

The household of faith was a critique of the family household. Often, one had to choose between these two families. In the early church, families were torn as the confession of Jesus demanded a response. Confessing Jesus provoked the core issue of loyalty. Which family would have the greater loyalty when Jesus said, "Follow me"? Clearly, the adopted family of God as Father had preeminence. Robert Hamerton-Kelly reminds us that Jesus modeled that choice as a child. He refers to the story in Luke 2. Mary and Joseph retraced the steps of their journey to look for Jesus. When they found him, Mary asked Jesus why he caused them so much anxiety. "He answered them, 'Why did you have to look for me? Didn't you know that I had to be in my Father's house?' " (Luke 2:49, TEV). Hamerton-Kelly says:

> The call of God the Father takes precedence over the summons of any earthly father; and justifies the breaking of family ties and the apparent neglect of natural obligations.

We know that people in the early church did deny family obligations and specifically denied the authority of the patriarch of the family. Elisabeth Schüssler Fiorenza quotes a wonderfully descriptive attack on this behavior of the Christians by Tacitus (*History*, v. 5) as one of many pieces of evidence to display the disruption in patriarchal families because of this new family. Tacitus realized the danger to Roman patriarchs of this new definition of the family:

> The earliest lesson they [Christians] receive is to despise the gods, to disown their country, and *to regard their parents, children and brothers as of little account* (italics mine).

Sometimes women converts deserted husbands or fathers to become evangelists, which must have been especially chilling, since women were not even potentially patriarchal replacements of the household father. The New Testament includes stories and hints of stories of men who left their father's house to become sons of the Father God. For example, James and John left their father, Zebedee (Mark 1:20); Peter acknowledges that everything (and presumably everybody) was left behind to follow Jesus (Mark 10:28–30).

There is a saying recorded in both Matthew (10:34–36) and Luke (12:51–53) which announces that Jesus brings into *that old family* not peace but a sword. It is into the patriarchal household presided over by a father with rights and responsibilities that the confession of Jesus brings enmity. For with Jesus there is a different definition of the family altogether. That new family is based precisely not on the rights and responsibilities of the father head of the household but on the intimate fatherhood of God. There is another saying, in Luke 11:27–28, which is paralleled in story form in Mark 3:31–35. In the Luke version, Jesus hears this blessing: "Blessed is the womb that bore you, and the breasts that you sucked." He responds, "Blessed rather are those who hear the word of God and keep it!" In the Mark story, Jesus received the message from his kinfolk, who wanted to see him. He responds, "Whoever does the will of God is my brother, and sister, and mother." His response in both cases underscores the primary loyalty to the family of faith *which has a different vision of what father means.*

The only person not specifically mentioned in this new family of discipleship is, in fact, father. Mothers are listed in the household of faith, but not fathers. God is the only father in the community of disciples. Whatever additional significance there may be in that fact, here is another implicit rejection of the claims of earthly patriarchal father power in favor of more of a shared power in the Spirit. It is the spirit that binds together the disciples, and the spirit is of God and the spirit is God. Since we cannot see God, the spirit is made known in Jesus, the special child of God who, as the Gospel of John says, is nearest to the Father's heart. Jesus prays that the disciples "be [one] in us; just as you [Father] are in me and I am in you" (John 17:21, TEV). One of the assumptions upon which this prayer is based is that the disciples participate in the same *stuff* that connects

God and Jesus. The same God that is in me is in the disciples, said Jesus. May the God in them be central, in charge, alive, as they live in the world. This is the same message Jesus gave to the woman at the well (John 4:21–24). God is spirit. Worship God in spirit and in truth. That woman becomes the adopted child into the new family of faith. She is held into relation with Jesus and all the other disciples by the spirit and becomes one of the early evangelists.

That new family is primary. That new family is at odds with the old family. All the children of the new family have access to their father through the spirit. That Father God is not the transcendent patriarch with rights and responsibilities. That Father God is an intimate, tender, present, available, compassionate, reliable Parent.

There is a saying of Jesus' that emphasizes the difference dramatically. "Call no man your father on earth, for you have one Father, who is in heaven" (Matt. 23:9). The passage is reminiscent of John the Baptist's call for repentance, which includes the denial of Abraham as father (Matt. 3:9). The saying is also clearly in the context of a critique of hierarchical religious authority and an assault on human privilege. The passage ends with this summary or conclusion: "The greatest one among you must be your servant. Whoever makes himself great will be humbled, and whoever humbles himself will be made great" (Matt. 23:11–12, TEV). This saying is a climax to an escalating rejection of patriarchal domination. Insofar as both Jesus and the disciples participate in God as spirit, there is a rejection of hierarchical family relationships. This rejection is further emphasized when no earthly father is named as participating in that spirit of the new family. Then for God alone to hold the name of father is "a critical subversion of all structures of domination" (Fiorenza, p. 151). There is good news in envisioning God as the only Father. There is not such good news, however, envisioning God only as the Father.

Many feminists, including Fiorenza, remind us in relation to this passage that the father represented here includes tenderness and compassion, characteristics associated with a woman. That does not help the exclusive male language. We could be tempted to fall back onto claiming tenderness and compassion as gender-specific (female) virtues.

Instead, we need to use this father symbol as a model for transforming human fathers and in no case presume that we have that model adequately available in earthly mothers. Here is the opportunity to strengthen father images and fathering behavior. God as Father is available. He is intimate. He is tender and compassionate. He suffers, leads, loves, recalls, forgives, reconciles, and starts over. He adopts children, especially orphans. He shares his own being-spirit with the children. And he never leaves them. He never ceases being a father. God the Father is reliable.

The advantages to this recovery of fathering are immense. Here is the critique of patriarchal domination and violence *within* a male symbol. Here is a model of what fathering is. Here is a challenge to human fathers. Here is a source of accountability for human fathering. For women to give up that reliable Father is to let patriarchal religion off the theological hook. To lose our Father God is to perpetuate our mourning and rage. Women's grief would be literally more creative by weeping over the anticipated death of dependencies, fear, and alienation. Bury the distorted father who represents all that. Instead, look for and insist upon the resurrection of the reliable Father.

The Bible may describe an attractive father God. That God is, in a special way, the Father of Jesus. And Jesus as the Christ is the central figure in our saving history. We are confronted with the inescapable reality: the Savior is in the form of the man, and only in the form of a man. What good news is there in that central symbol for women?

5

Jesus the Model

In Alice Walker's *The Color Purple,* one sister writes to another, quoting a friend:

> When I found out I thought God was white, and a man, I lost interest. You mad cause he don't seem to listen to your prayers. Humph! Do the mayor listen to anything colored say? Ask Sofia, she say.
>
> But I don't have to ast Sofia. I know white people never listen to colored, period. If they do, they only listen long enough to be able to tell you what to do.

That same letter begins, "I don't write to God no more. I write to you." This Black woman turns away from the alienating and oppressive image of the white man God to the reassurance of the Black sister.

There are many theological messages in this letter. Among them is the message stated with simple eloquence in the first sentence: "When I found out I thought God was white, and a man, I lost interest." There is something so fundamentally human in envisioning God as like us. We need to be sure that God understands, listens, and responds. To image God as the one who is not only very different from me but as one who enslaves me is intolerable. No minimally healthy person will continue to "write" to that kind of god. That image of God will be either rejected in some way or changed in some way. In this case the white man God is rejected by utter indifference.

The image of God could be enlarged instead. There are ways to image God as like us. God is so vast that all the colors and sexes and nationalities and vocations and an infinite list of attributes and experience can make a connection with humankind.

The Maleness of Jesus

It is not so with Jesus. We can look for all the qualities that remind us of Black, or Latin, or female. All the looking and connecting will not change the person Jesus. He was a man. For that reason alone it is tempting to put aside this powerful male symbol altogether. Then women can get on with affirming our own authority. Some of those who do not put him aside, however, rightly assess his power for liberation and partly for that reason continue to deal with "The Man."

It is important to ask the question of the maleness of Jesus for at least two reasons. The first is a tactical one. Most of those who positively appreciate the maleness of Jesus do so in order to preserve male privilege. To permit the preservers of male privilege to "own" the man who is also a liberator is a tactical blunder. Whether Jesus the man is the complete symbol or the only symbol of liberation is not the point. He does represent for many of us a dangerous remembrance. We appropriate his story as yet another Exodus story. We remember that God does not intend any kind of slavery for us. We recall Jesus as representative of the underclass. There is another aspect to the tactical issue. Jesus is still authoritative also for many other women who may not now see him as a liberator but who will turn to none other as the vital source of faith and hope. These women help fill the churches and do their duties, informed by a misogyny that distorts Jesus as an excuse to exploit women. It is for the sake of these two different companies of women, both the dangerous and the docile, that the man inside the Christ must be taken seriously.

A second reason for exploring the maleness of Jesus is a historical one. Jesus is the most influential person in Christian corporate religious history and therefore informs our present and future. Some who reject him do so as a straightforward selection of other historical models. They look to "secular" history or to women's history to find heroes and hope. They understand history as the context for imaging and creating new things. On the other hand, some who reject Jesus border on an escape from history altogether and run the risk of not engaging the hard contextual realities of this world. Much of the appeal to the Goddess is an appeal to a mythical past or an expectant future. A mythical past or a future fantasy may, indeed, help women create a vision and stretch into something new. Myth and fantasy can also support distracted dreaming and abstract religion. In any case, a flight from history is not possible; history sets the possibilities and limits of change. History itself cannot be changed, but it can be redeemed. First, however, it must be accepted on its own terms. And the maleness of Jesus is one of those terms.

What then of Jesus?

The one special incarnation closest to the Father's heart who is confessed as Savior walked the earth as a man. The central Christian symbol for the fullness of humanity was male. The Christian symbol for the fullness of reconciliation between God and people was male.

The maleness of Jesus is a stumbling block to many women, first of all because he is not like us. He is a stumbling block also to many women who view him as one more oppressive male symbol at the heart of a long tradition of oppressive male symbols. Nancy Van Vuuren's statement catches this sense of oppression:

> The coming of the messiah did not liberate women. God became definitely male in *his* incarnation, Jesus, and he used the body of a woman to allow himself to become incarnate.

There is a problem for women being "saved" by any male intermediary, whether that intermediary is a husband, a priest, a theologian, or Jesus, because under the conditions of patriarchy the intermediary has power over the woman. He can block access to the throne of grace. He can invent conditions out of his own self-interest by which we would be permitted the means of saving grace. And that in fact has happened. Women became defined in the Western church in relationship to men. Women were restricted to service vocations in house or church. Women could be wife-mothers or sister-mothers, both helpers to the fathers. The Eucharist and church membership has been withheld from uncompliant women. Clergymen may still withhold the Eucharist from women as punishment for our desire to control our own bodies. Clergymen may still send wives back to battering husbands, wondering what the wives did wrong to provoke such wrath. The more typical contemporary manner of punishing women is simply to ignore us in language, liturgy, and leadership until we just lose interest.

Now, we cannot blame all of that on Jesus! At the same time, we have to acknowledge that any male figure under the conditions of patriarchy is a structured-in temptation for abuse. One of the historic abuses is the patriarchal argument that there is an inherent connection between the authority of Jesus and the authority of other earthly men. The Vatican Doctrinal Congregation's "Declaration on the Question of the Admission of Women to the Ministerial Priesthood," October 15, 1976, is a prototype of this view. The Declaration argues that since a priest truly acts in the place of Christ, there should be that "natural resemblance" between Christ and his minister. Rosemary Ruether's critique of this view in *To Change the World* is delightfully stinging:

> Since this strange new version of the imitation of Christ does not exclude a Negro, a Chinese, or a Dutchman from repre-

senting a first-century Jew, or a wealthy prelate from representing a carpenter's son, or sinners from representing the savior,
we must assume this imitation of Christ has now been reduced
to one essential element, namely, male sex.

This doctrine has a misogynist history and is based on
the presumptions of the maleness of God and the maleness
of humanity as normative. There are Roman Catholic
theologians who have condemned this doctrine as hereti-
cal. The question remains: Can Christ be liberated from
male privilege under the conditions of patriarchy?

We could name this doctrine in all of its manifestations
as an excuse for male privilege and dismiss it. We could just
deny the rights of earthly intermediaries. Two facts remain. First, he is not like us in this one important respect.
Our sexuality and the life experience that accompanies our
sexuality cannot be identified with Jesus. We do not have
the level of comfort of "writing" to a sister. Second, because
he is linked with maleness he will continue to be linked with
male privilege. Therefore, for Jesus to be an appropriate
saving symbol for women, we would, it seems to me, have
to overcome these problems somehow. Let us take up each
of them.

First, he is not like us. Once again we are confronted
with the scandal of particularity. That the vastness and
holiness of God should be specially incarnate in any one
particular concrete human being in any one particular time
in any one particular place is an affront on the one hand to
the majesty of God. On the other hand, that incarnation is
an embarrassment to those least like the incarnate one.

The missionary movement of the early church had to
contend with a world for whom the cross was a symbol of
earthliness, death, and failure. That did not seem God-like
at all. That Jesus was a Jew was and continues to be a
scandal to Gentile Christians. Anglo-Americans deny or
distance ourselves from the Jewish Jesus. Many of us grew
up with a Nordic Jesus displayed in Sunday school pictures

and a clear message that Jesus was "better than" or "different from" other Jews: that is, not *really* Jewish. Now we are aware of another scandal of particularity. We are faced with the particularity of the maleness of Jesus as a man. There is at the very least some comfort associated with the fact that this is one more discrete particularity in a long list of particularities which the church has engaged before. The particularity of Jesus is more than a comfort, however. The special, particular incarnation is also an affirmation of nitty-gritty mundane history. It is a way of saying that God does not hide out from history but is in the middle of it. It is a way of saying that earthliness, death, and failure are exactly some of the things that are God-like for they happen in human history. Christians stand in awe of the sheer movement of history, partly because of the centrality and intimacy of this incarnation. The scandal of particularity is both a comfort and an affirmation of our histories.

Still, one wonders why. Why was that special incarnation like *them* and not like *us?* One of the "solutions" to this problem is to ignore or minimize the maleness of Jesus. One of the ways to minimize the maleness of Jesus is to make the clear distinction between Jesus as man and Jesus as the Christ. That distinction is especially important in this historical situation, as the women's movement continues to press the church on many fronts. One of those fronts is the ordination of women, which of course is directly connected to the full humanity of women. (There is no such thing as both equality and role exclusion. If women are fully human, we can do anything any humans do.) The Vatican's Declaration in particular provoked commentary on the distinction between Jesus as man and Jesus as the Christ as an argument for the ordination of women. R. A. Norris, Jr., was one who reviewed doctrinal history and persuasively concluded that the tradition behind the Declaration was a modern invention, whereas in the "Fathers . . . the maleness of Jesus is of no Christological interest." The distinction between Jesus as male and Jesus as the Christ is an important distinction to make, not only on behalf of the ordination of women but also on behalf of the humanity of both women and men and on behalf of the catholicity of Christ's saving power. Nevertheless, the historical Jesus remains in the form of a man. That fact and that memory continue to tempt men to arrogance and privilege. To distinguish Jesus from Savior is important, and we need to keep faith with the difference. It does not satisfy female longing or prevent male temptations.

The most typical way of minimizing Jesus' maleness is to concentrate on his androgyny. Jesus is viewed as both male and female. The argument is that he holds in his personality characteristics of both the sexes. Therefore, he can represent both of the sexes and is model for humanity. In this approach we would need to reenvision Jesus as perfect person. Virginia Ramey Mollenkott puts it this way:

> The whole issue concerning modern women's representation by and in Christ is solved by the realization that Jesus is clearly depicted in the Bible not as a male but as an androgyne. That is, he is pictured as a human being in whom "masculine" and "feminine" characteristics are harmoniously mingled. He is Perfect Humanity.

One could concentrate on the humanity of Jesus and even note what has traditionally been called female in the life of Jesus. According to the Gospel of Luke, Jesus himself uses female images pertaining to God and himself. God is like the woman who loses a coin and searches tenaciously until she finds it. Then she celebrates with her neighbors and friends. That is the way God seeks out lost people and rejoices over their repentance and return (Luke 15:3–10). Jesus is like the mother hen who gathers the chicks under her wings. That is what Jesus longs to do for the children of Jerusalem (Luke 13:34). Jesus may also have referred to himself as female in the Gospel of John, as the one who satisfies the thirsty from inside himself, from his own body (John 7:37–39). Whether he did or not, he did—like a woman?—offer refreshment for the parched tongues and dirty feet. Jesus also offered his own tears. It's okay for men to cry.

The appeal to androgyny has additional precedent in the tradition. Dame Julian of Norwich is one from the medieval mystical tradition who has been rediscovered and appreciated by feminist theologians. Dame Julian viewed Jesus as both mother and father and called to him in those names. As mother, Jesus feeds us from his body. In the early church, many Gnostics viewed Jesus and God—and people—as both male and female. Their view of androgyny was in fact one of the things that frightened the patriarchs in the early church and led to their rejection of gnosticism as an integral part of the official tradition. The patriarchs wanted to make a clear distinction between male and female. They did not want to blur the sexes.

Such determination to separate clearly male and female reminds me of the current speeches that begin: "I believe in equal pay for equal work *but* . . . " Those speeches end with *"Vive la différence!"* Preoccupation with sex differentiation is inherently oppressive. "Different from" becomes "better than." "Different from" becomes "Mothers are the real parents." Women also behave oppressively under the rubric of "different is better." In everyday language and situations, women exchange complaints—about *them*. "All of them are insensitive." "Men are such babies!" It could be argued, then, that virtually any means of blurring the sexes counts against this oppression and helps liberation. Androgyny does in a particular way blur distinctions and points to a common humanity. Furthermore, androgyny is relatively popular right now. Is there any reason *not* to embrace androgyny?

I believe there is very good reason to be critical of androgyny. That reason is, ironically, the same reason for criticizing the preoccupation with sex differentiation. The same dynamic is operative in both situations. "Male" and "female" characteristics are isolated in both cases. Putting those characteristics inside one body still keeps them separated and encourages the alienations from oneself and others. How does naming Jesus "feminine" help me as a woman? Or, to put it another way, If Jesus is both male and female in one body as "perfect humanity," there is *no* way a woman or woman symbol can be anything but imperfect humanity. "Perfect humanity" has already been defined in the context of male biology. I believe that viewing gender as irrelevant will take us all farther along with fewer dangers than the viewing of gender as differentiated, whether that differentiation is in biological or psychological categories.

To return to the illustration of androgyny in the early church on whether the sexes were highly differentiated or blurred. There is a third alternative. Gender was irrelevant. Fiorenza (pp. 208–218) describes the importance of the baptismal formula as reconstructed in Galatians 3:26–28.

> You are all [children] of God, through faith. For as many of you as were baptized into Christ have put on Christ. There is neither Jew nor Greek, there is neither slave nor free, there is neither male nor female; for you are all one.

All factions used the same language. Did "there is neither male nor female" mean blurring of the sexes or separation of the sexes or neither? What did "put on Christ" mean? Similar language is used throughout the New Testament. There is the "new person" or the "new nature" or "renewed after the image of the Creator" or being "clothed in Christ." This was important language to represent the newness of the faith, the reality of conversion, the connection with Christ's spirit, and a symbol of the new covenant. Like the symbol of "breaking down the barriers," these symbols more likely point to the breaking of the barriers of race and sex. They just have no significance any more. The argument by androgynists that describes Jesus' "femininity" does make a connection with us but not the connection of female characteristics inside a male body. The richness and variety of Jesus' personality and behavior help make a human connection, not a gender connection. Whether the man is "softened" or "helped" by so-called female characteristics or not, a male body houses all the images and characteristics.

Partly for those reasons, some feminists look for a female incarnation as the appropriate saving symbol for women. That female incarnation is sometimes androgynous and sometimes not. There is also precedent in the tradition for the female incarnation. In a part of the medieval church that believed in the advent of the feminine spirit, two groups did not look for the female incarnation because they believed they had already found her, in Prous Boneta (early fourteenth century) and Guglielma (c. 1271). In the nineteenth century, the Shaker leader Mother Ann Lee was also named as an incarnation. Perhaps she was the singular incarnation designated as such in the modern period. The image and search for a female messianic figure, however, was not singular. A variety of freethinkers in the nineteenth century looked for a female messiah. Some of them believed that the female was the "superior" of the two incarnations. Others believed that female characteristics wherever and however manifested were superior. The trend toward viewing females as religiously superior was part of a larger historical development which was aided and abetted by the first wave of feminism. Most leaders of the first wave argued that it was precisely because women were spiritually and morally superior that they were needed in public life. "Superior" means more loving, tender, just, and moral. These were women's qualities that were needed to clean up the marketplace. Antifeminists tended to state the same belief and argued for different results. Either women's morals were too tender for the rough-and-tumble marketplace or their superiority was needed at home to tame the beast there and teach the next generation a better way.

There has been no advantage for women in a view of our superiority. For us to affirm superiority is a strategic blunder. In the past, "superiority" has not really meant superior at all. Female "superiority" has dramatically restricted women's work choices to service industries of one form or another. We must either clean up the house or clean up the hospital (government, business, whatever). Moral superiority has not fitted us for the tough decisions, so we could not possibly be in charge of the hospital (government, business, whatever). Emotional superiority has confined us in interpersonal relationships also. We are more understanding. Therefore we are more forgiving. Therefore, they can afford to be more abusive. Superiority has meant a specific set of designations and characteristics which are *autonomically* confining, however one values them. Under the conditions of patriarchy, preoccupation with differences between the sexes will continue to oppress. Women are equally capable of oppressing. All we have lacked is equal opportunity. We don't need a female divinity or the equal rights amendment because women are better. We need our religious and public place just because we are. The superiority of women or men is a virulent form of sexual differentiation that is inherently confining, alienating, and abusive.

The most helpful approach to ignoring or minimizing the maleness of Jesus is to concentrate on his activity and function as Liberator. In that way he stands in the prophetic tradition in solidarity with other humans called to a vocation of justice and liberation. He also represents the authentic Word of God demonstrable in his life as servant which overturns privilege of any kind, including male privilege. So it is that Rosemary Ruether (in *Sexism and God-Talk*) views the maleness of Jesus as having "no ultimate significance." Rather, Jesus announces a new humanity and engages in new relationships. Jesus is the Christ as "the representative of liberated humanity and the liberating Word of God." . . . Jesus as Christ models and points to a different kind of community where leadership is not tied to power over another. Leadership has to do with mutuality and service. In this new community there is a "revolution of relationships." As Jesus modeled in his own behavior the leadership of servant, there is in some sense an overcoming of transcendent hierarchical power. God broke through patriarchy. We have a glimpse then into God's new thing, but that new thing was not and could not be realized under the conditions of patriarchy. For Ruether, Christ is not necessarily male, and the maleness of Jesus is irrelevant.

There is much to commend this approach to the man Jesus. According to the tradition, Jesus can readily be seen as nonpatriarchal. Jesus takes the initiative as a man who contradicts male privilege. Jesus contradicts any kind of privilege of one human over another. Jesus was feminist and liberator. Jesus' feminism is increasingly documented by feminist theologians. Let us summarize some of those discoveries. Jesus used stories about both women and men to communicate his teachings about God. He also radicalized particular teachings about women. One of his teachings protected the rights of wives through the sayings on monogamy, divorce, and adultery. Jesus healed women, including unclean taboo women. He conversed with them, taught them, ate with them, shared his messianic secret with them, appeared first to them after the resurrection, and commissioned them disciples and evangelists. Considering the patriarchal attitude and behavior toward women in Jesus' day, it is significant that stories of his solidarity with and intercession for them survived in the church. Considering also the compromises with male privilege made by the early church, it is doubly significant that the witness to Jesus as a feminist and liberator survived.

Jesus' feminism and the egalitarianism of the Jesus movement were compromised in the early church. Why and how that happened is another story. What is important here is that there is a credible witness to the contradictions to any form of patriarchal privilege and the affirmations of women and all the poor and powerless by Jesus and by much of the early church.

Still the question returns. A woman can be a feminist too. A woman can treat women and men well. A woman can represent liberation also. A woman can renounce all systems of oppression. Jesus' feminism and liberation is to the advantage of women; his sex is not. Or, as Mary Daly succinctly puts it in *Beyond God the Father* (p. 73), "Jesus was a feminist, but so what?" We have still not identified any positive interpretative value on the maleness itself. We must affirm the common humanity as a key identification between ourselves and Jesus. We must affirm also the danger of preoccupation with or thinking "first in terms of his male sex or his racial origin" as "biological determinism" (Letty Russell). We may not think "first" of his sex, but we will get around to thinking about it. And when we do, we are left with valuable qualifications and arguments. We are also left, however, with no specific advantage in his maleness for us, and the disadvantage of a patriarchal excuse for abuse remains. Is such a positive value necessary? Is such a positive value possible?

The Model Maker for Men

Inside the view of Jesus as Liberator there is, I believe, an implicit advantage *for women* to the maleness of Jesus. One of the ways Jesus modeled a revolution in relationships was by becoming himself a servant. Unlike women, he did not *have to be a servant*. He had power and access to power. But he gave it up! Jesus thereby modeled in his own being the dramatic assault on male privilege. Who but a man could credibly teach and model such a revolution in relationships by giving up power? Only a man could do that, because only men had power. Jesus' maleness is neither a weakness in the story nor is it irrelevant. The maleness of Jesus is a strongpoint in the story of giving up power and becoming a servant, joining the underclass of women and other servants in order to abolish servitude altogether. If Jesus' maleness is seen as restricting redemption, then the servanthood model is missing the key point. If servanthood is a key point, then maleness is an essential asset. This historical man modeled a transformation of power that gave credibility to his teachings. Jesus refused to pick up the kind of kingly patriarchal power even in the face of his own agony and death. Having emptied himself of the power of God to become a servant, Jesus remained faithful to his vocation "unto death, even death on the cross" (Phil. 2:8). According to the apostle Paul, it was precisely for that reason that Jesus is the Christ: "Therefore God has highly exalted him" (Phil. 2:9). Becoming Christ was not dependent upon the maleness of Jesus, but the maleness of Jesus became an asset in a credible transformation of power.

By contrast, Daly in *Gyn/Ecology* criticizes the cross as a thoroughly patriarchal symbol. What she notices in the cross is "typical" male violence and death. The tree is normally so alive and full of color. It is a source of food and comfort. Here at the cross, the tree is itself dead and has been perverted into an instrument of death. Jesus suffers and dies on the dead tree. Daly argues that violence and death are essential to patriarchal religion. Her argument is refuted by clear themes in the ministry and passion of Jesus. Jesus died partly because he was *not* a patriarch. Jesus died partly because he brought the prophetic tradition to bear on patriarchal institutions, even the family. Jesus died partly because he was a troublemaker within his own precious patriarchal community.

Even Marcion, a church father of the second century, agrees. He attributes Jesus' death to the fact that he led the children and women astray. He did not behave the way patriarchs behave. He gave up his patriarchal power. Violence and killing may be patriarchal symbols, but Jesus refused to take up another patriarchal symbol to save

himself. His death is for the death of patriarchy. The cross
is more credibly a symbol for the death of patriarchy than
a symbol for the celebration of violence and killing. The
death of a powerful man is an appropriate representation
of the death of patriarchy. We have already noted the
powerful baptismal formula of Galatians 3:25–28. The
language is connected with breaking the barriers. Everyone was a child of God.

Imagine the underclass hearing those words at their
baptism. What they heard was the declaration of the end of
racism, sexism, and classism. What they heard was a
credible witness to the presence and teachings of Jesus of
Nazareth. The powerful baptism formula did not depend
on the maleness of Jesus. But the baptism formula had a
particular credibility *because of* the maleness of Jesus. For
the free man, Jesus demonstrated servant behavior *for other
free men.* These men, too, could shed tears and wash feet.
These men, too, would have to learn that they were called
not to power and privilege but to service. No, James and
John could not sit on either side of Jesus like some
lieutenants or princes. Instead, they could follow Jesus'
example, who "came not to be served but to serve, and to
give his life" (Matt. 20:28). When Jesus preached servanthood and humility he was preaching to the brothers. The
brothers were in the synagogue. The brothers were more
easily physically close to him in public. Furthermore, that
servanthood was a calling. Humility was a matter of choice.
Men were the ones who could make that choice. The cost
of service and humility was demonstrated by our brother,
Jesus. At the beginning of his ministry, Jesus' first declaration was to overturn privilege. The man spoke the words of
abolition to other men (Luke 4:18–19). At the end, the
resurrected Jesus tried one last time to get his message to
those "foolish men" who still didn't get it (Luke 24:25). In
one sense, Jesus had a particular kind of ministry with men
and a particularly persuasive way of representing that
ministry in himself.

The advantage of a male savior is the judgment on patriarchy itself through the presence of this model maker for men. One key content to that modeling is the yielding of power. Jesus infuses other men with the power to give up power. Instead of minimizing Jesus' maleness or pronouncing it irrelevant, we need to use it to hold men's feet to the fire. If powerful men want to continue to identify themselves with the man Jesus, then let them. And let them also then give up their power and become just folks. We can remind contemporary patriarchs of the cost of male identification with the Savior. Those costs have more to do with the story of the rich young ruler (Matt. 19:16–22) than it does the image of a transcendent *Lord*. The rich young ruler was challenged by Jesus to *relinquish* his riches, not *justify* them. Similarly, modern patriarchs may not justify power by linking up with the power of Jesus.

The early church somehow held on to this model maker even as it began to compromise its liberating gospel and fall into a hierarchical institution. The Ephesian letter, for example, has the most comprehensive record of the household code in the New Testament (Eph. 5:21—6:9). The household code was a collection or list of rights and responsibilities within the patriarchal family. These New Testament versions seem to be a compromise between the starkest power arrangements on the one hand, with women viewed as property, and the liberating gospel on the other hand. The language of wives' submission in that context is still ambiguous in that there is mutuality expected of the marriage partners. The model maker for men had intruded at least that much. (The only unqualifiedly sexist passage is 1 Timothy 2:11–15. In that passage, women are blamed for the fall into sin and may not teach or tell a man what to do. Its vehemence against women in leadership is another indication that women were in fact exercising leadership.) Nevertheless, the hierarchy of the household code is real.

I remember pondering that part of Ephesians one sleepless night until I jumped out of bed and reread that wives were to regard husbands *as they regard the Lord.* Then I turned back to the Philippian hymn in order to answer this question: *And who is that Lord?* A man who did not "try to become equal with God" but "gave up all he had, and took the nature of a servant" (Phil. 2:6–7, TEV). In the darkness I shouted to absolutely no one at all, "If I find me that kind of a man I will reconsider!" That was a little frivolous. But in the cold light of day (as they say), the basic insight held up. The household code is in the context of a new creation before and beyond Ephesians which had already broken into the world in Jesus Christ. Jesus. A man who gave up power. The model "Lord" of the household of faith is neither a taskmaster nor a benevolent despot. The model Lord of the household is a servant.

The strategic implication is that women need not be alone on the way to liberation. If this one man can empty himself of a power far greater than the power of money and status, surely some men with mere money or status can give up a part of that lesser power. In any event, men are held accountable on the basis of their own faith and identification with that one man. Holding powerful people accountable to their own rules and rationale has integrity and is frequently strategically helpful.

Martin Luther King was one who did not invent new rules and rationales for abolishing racism. He used his religious heritage and the democratic tradition as having already established the content of justice. What he did do was hold this country accountable to its own inheritance. You call yourself an American? You say you are a Christian? Well, this is what that means.

The maleness of Jesus is an asset as a model maker for men. He judges patriarchy through self-giving in his life and ministry. The first way is by giving up power. Jesus calls other men to give up the power of male privilege.

A second way that Jesus is a model maker for men is in his support of and presence to women. We have already summarized Jesus' behavior as friend and advocate. Because he is a model, it is the quality of his friendship that is important. Often the illustrations of Jesus' relationships with and feelings about women are collected as views and behavior which establish justice for women. That is, Jesus was a model breaker for women. In short, he was a feminist, but so what? The so-what question remains because the interpretation of Jesus as feminist focuses on women. The so-whatness in his friendships has more to do with what he modeled for *men* in those situations. Jesus was really present to women. He was not absent in the ways that most fathers are absent. Jesus was both physically available and emotionally present. He allowed himself openness and vulnerability. He demonstrated the capacity for intimacy. He shared himself. Jesus was about self-disclosure, refusing the male habits of privacy and distance.

Several studies would indicate that married women are more likely to suffer mental ill health than either their husbands or single women. In the United States the married man is the happiest of his sex, but the married woman is the unhappiest of hers. The emotional support available to husbands and withheld from wives is a key explanation behind these data. Gail Sheehy in *Passages* is one of many who records the tendency in men over thirty to achieve competence and control at the expense of tenderness and concern for the development of their families.

Eugene Bianchi argues that another way men create distance from women is through "psychic celibacy" in which husbands are sexually present but emotionally absent. Bianchi also describes the football game illustration of machismo in such a way that it sounds like a preparation or a way to stay in training for "psychic celibacy." We know that many football terms are used as double entendres for sexual behavior, especially male aggression. When both football and sexual intercourse are imaged as a game with goals for the male players to accomplish, the object of the game becomes just that: an object. Emotional distance is maintained. Jesus may have been sexually absent but he was emotionally present. In contrast to male privacy and distance stand the memory of Jesus' presence, affection, support, and intimacy.

He was moved by the Syrophoenician woman and turned against his own stated task in order to heal her daughter and acknowledge her faith (Mark 7:24–30). He pitied the widow of Nain, reaching out to her with kind words and the raising of her only son (Luke 7:11–17). He named the bent-over woman daughter of Abraham, including her into the inner family circle (Luke 13:10–17). He was touched—literally—by the love of the penitent woman (Luke 7:36–50). He was accessible to Peter's mother-in-law, whom he healed (Luke 4:38–39). He engaged the Samaritan woman at the well (John 4:1–42). He grieved with Mary and Martha over the death of Lazarus, whom he raised (John 11:1–44). He also gave these women friends support not only in that sorrow but in the vocation of learning (Luke 10:38–42).

The strategic implication for women is to raise expectations in their relationships with men and refuse to settle for privacy and distance. Excuses will not do. We may understand that men have been socialized for emotional absence. We may understand some of the ways in which it is difficult for men to learn availability and presence. But they will have to learn. Because, this side of the Jesus model, we will not settle for objectification or psychic celibacy or emotional absence or distance. We will not settle for it partly by changing our own expectations. Expectations have something to do with results. Behavioral sciences now know what the women's movement and primary-school teachers have known for a long time: If one expects quality from another person, that person will try to give it. To that extent we participate in the behaviors of others.

Jesus is a model maker for men as present to women. He

calls men to give up privacy and distance. Jesus is a model maker for men by the giving of his presence to women.

This presence is not what some radical feminists observe in the Mary-Martha story of Luke 10:38–42. What these feminists notice, instead, is that Mary is listening at the feet of Jesus. She is seen as dependent on a man, as women always are. The only thing that has changed in this approach is the environment. The arena for her traditional role has simply changed from the kitchen to the study. Again, in this story, let us again concentrate on what Jesus is doing. What is there about him as a model maker for men? Jesus is teacher. Mary is studying with this rabbi. That is the meaning of sitting at his feet. Competent teachers share wisdom with students because both wisdom and students are treasured. Competent teachers also engage students as colleagues by asking and listening as well as answering and speaking. The teacher is one of the happiest portraits of Jesus.

He used the question-and-answer method. To the woman taken in adultery: "Has no one condemned you?" "No one sir." "Neither do I." He pressed people to reflect. On prostitutes and tax gatherers entering the Kingdom: "What do you think? A man had two sons. . . . " He told stories: "Well, there was this persistent widow. . . ." He used the past to enlighten the present: "You have heard, and read of old. . . . " He gave examples: "The kingdom is like . . . " He used history and stories. The history was a common history. His "students" knew it and respected it. The stories came from common ordinary living. His "students" would understand them.

Thank God Jesus was not a systematic theologian!

When we concentrate on Jesus as a model maker for men, there is a vision of the sharing of one of the great sources of empowerment: knowledge, especially self-knowledge. Jesus shared his most treasured self-knowledge with Martha when he told her that he was the resurrection. Similarly he disclosed himself to the woman at the well. Finally, he disclosed himself to Mary, who knew him when he called her by name. The man Jesus was a teacher who shared his knowledge with women. As a model maker for men, Jesus again represents a judgment on patriarchy through the self-giving of his knowledge.

"Let my people know" is a powerful demand, for knowledge is power. The strategic implication for women is to recognize and acquire the necessary knowledge about ourselves and patriarchal structures. Without that knowledge we cannot enter, criticize, or challenge ourselves or those structures.

The maleness of Jesus, then, has positive value in the judgment of patriarchy and its strategic implications for change when one sees him as a model maker for men in at least these three areas of self-giving: power, presence, and knowledge. It is appropriate that a male savior "speak" this direct word to men. It is also appropriate for women to keep pointing to Jesus as a model for manhood.

Jesus the Model Breaker

Jesus is also a model breaker for women. As a model maker he judges patriarchy; as a model breaker he also transcends patriarchy. He transcends it through the medium of experience. Jesus trusted his own experience. That transcending of the constraints of patriarchy is dangerous to the status quo when it is used by anybody. Women affirm and use experience in a variety of ways as data for theological reflection. We trust our experience over against inherited patriarchal constraints of doctrine, law, and ecclesiastical organization. We decide out of our cumulative experience what is valid and revelatory in the tradition. (Of course, listening and reading the tradition becomes part of our experience also.) We decide what is valid and revelatory in the present. We use our experience as reliable and as necessary to the full witness of faith. Often we turn to our experience against a doctrinal ecclesiology which is determined to set the parameters of valid discovery and discernment.

It is more than a little comforting that Jesus pushed out his parameter of inherited truth. Jesus grasped his own authority and pushed it to such limits that he was accused of blasphemy and insurrection. Jesus' teaching methods illustrate the care for and the power of human experience. His answer to John's inquiry—"Are you the one who is to come?"—illustrates his confidence in the authority of experience. He answers, "Go and tell . . . what you hear and see" (Matt. 11:3–4, NEB). Trust your experience and share it!

Jesus is a model breaker for women by appealing to his own experience of the holy and his own vocation. That message does not call on women to absolutize Jesus' experience but to emulate it. We, too, need to transcend the patriarchal parameters of authority through reaching into our own experience for the data of spiritual formation. Nelle Morton's imagery of the "divine act" of "hearing to speech" by "a prior great Listening Ear" is a helpful image for women who are routinely interrupted and silenced. Women can be helped into our own authentic speech by the same God who empowered Jesus into his own authentic Word. That Word pressed at the boundaries of inherited religion. That Word pressed at the boundaries of status quo politics. The strategic implication is to hold to this dangerous remembrance for the purpose of maintaining integrity and mobilizing courage.

Jesus is the one utterly reliable man in the lives of many women. Jesus is our hope. He eschews the power and distance of patriarchy. He also transcends patriarchy, by taking seriously his own experiential authority. Jesus shows us how to reach inside ourselves and trust our experience. He is a man who is fully present to us. The maleness of

Jesus is not the primary word, but it is a positive word. That Word delivers a judgment on patriarchy through model making for men as self-giving of power, presence, and knowledge.

Afterword

*Turn the hearts of fathers
to their children—Malachi 4:6; Luke 1:17*

Fathering is a mark of prophetic expectation. Fathering is a mark of a redeemed community. The Christian community is without excuse for contributing to the absence or perversions of fathering. The Christian community must at minimum reorder its own life to give priority to fathering.

I believe that fathering is essential to our survival. Caring fathers are less likely to drop bombs, tolerate hunger, or excuse poverty. For that reason, fathering is not only a matter of prophetic expectation, it is a matter of prophetic urgency. We do not have the time to hope that some future generation will turn things around. We will have to find the ways to intrude into the present.

List of Works Cited

Banks, Louis, *The Motherhood of God* (Eaton and Mains, 1901).

Bianchi, Eugene C., "Psychic Celibacy and the Quest for Mutuality," in Rosemary Ruether and Eugene C. Bianchi, *From Machismo to Mutuality: Man–Woman Liberation in America* (Paulist Press, 1976).

Bos, Joanna, "When You Pray Say Our Father" (*Presbyterian Survey*, May 1981), pp. 10–12.

Christ, Carol P., "Spiritual Quest and Women's Experience" and "Why Women Need the Goddess: Phenomenological, Psychological, and Political Reflections," in *Womanspirit Rising: A Feminist Reader in Religion*, ed. Carol P. Christ and Judith Plaskow (Harper & Row, 1979), pp. 228–245 and 273–287.

Cottle, Thomas J., "A Father Dead or Alive" (*Christianity and Crisis*, June 9, 1980).

Daly, Mary, *Beyond God the Father: Toward a Philosophy of Women's Liberation* (Beacon Press, 1973), pp. 19, 73.

————, *Gyn/Ecology: The Metaethics of Radical Feminism* (Beacon Press, 1978).

Dinnerstein, Dorothy, *The Mermaid and the Minotaur: Sexual Arrangements and Human Malaise* (Harper & Row, 1976).

Fiorenza, Elisabeth Schüssler, *In Memory of Her: A Feminist Theological Reconstruction of Christian Origins* (Crossroad, 1983), pp. 151, 208–218, 264.

Freud, Sigmund, "Some Psychological Consequences of the Anatomical Distinctions Between the Sexes" (1925).

Gearhart, Sally Miller, "The Spiritual Dimension: Death and Resurrection of a Hallelujah Dyke," in *Our Right to Love: A*

Lesbian Resource Book, ed. Ginny Vida (Prentice-Hall, 1978).

Gilligan, Carol, *In a Different Voice: Psychological Theory and Woman's Development* (Harvard University Press, 1982).

Goldenberg, Naomi R., *Changing of the Gods: Feminism and the End of Traditional Religions* (Beacon Press, 1979).

Goldstein, Valerie Saiving, "The Human Situation: A Feminine View," in *The Nature of Man in Theological and Psychological Perspective,* ed. Simon Doniger (Harper & Row, 1962).

Gross, Rita, "The Second Coming of the Goddess" (*Anima,* Fall 1979), pp. 48–59.

Hamerton-Kelly, Robert, *God the Father: Theology and Patriarchy in the Teaching of Jesus* (Fortress Press, 1979), p. 65.

Lyles, Jean Caffey, "The God-Language Bind" (*The Christian Century,* April 16, 1980), p. 431.

Mollenkott, Virginia Ramey, "The Androgyny of Jesus" (*Daughters of Sarah,* March 1976), p. 4.

Morley, Janet, in *Cross Currents* (Fall 1982), p. 314.

Morton, Nelle, "Preaching the Word," in *Sexist Religion and Women in the Church, No More Silence!,* ed. Alice L. Hageman (Association Press, 1974), p. 134.

Norris, R. A., Jr., "The Ordination of Women and the Maleness of Christ" (*Supplementary Series of the Anglican Theological Review,* June 1976).

Pagels, Elaine, *The Gnostic Gospels* (Random House, 1979), p. 142.

Plaskow, Judith, *Sex, Sin, and Grace: Women's Experience and the Theologies of Reinhold Niebuhr and Paul Tillich* (University Press of America, 1980), p. 151.

Rich, Adrienne, *On Lies, Secrets, and Silence: Selected Prose 1966–1978* (W. W. Norton & Co., 1979), p. 221.

Ruether, Rosemary, *Sexism and God-Talk: Toward a Feminist Theology* (Beacon Press, 1983), p. 137.

——, *To Change the World: Christology and Cultural Criticism* (Crossroad, 1981).

——, "Why Males Fear Women Priests" (*Witness,* Summer 1980).

Russell, Letty, *Human Liberation in a Feminist Perspective—A Theology* (Westminster Press, 1974), pp. 138–139.

Sheehy, Gail, *Passages* (E. P. Dutton & Co., 1976).

Soelle, Dorothee, "Mysticism, Liberation, and the Names of God" (*Christianity and Crisis,* June 22, 1981).

Strasser, Susan, *Never Done: A History of American Housework* (Pantheon Books, 1982).

Trible, Phyllis, *God and the Rhetoric of Sexuality* (Fortress Press, 1978), p. 45.

Van Vuuren, Nancy, *The Subversion of Women as Practiced by Church, Witch-Hunters, and Other Sexists* (Westminster Press, 1973), p. 26.

Walker, Alice, *The Color Purple* (Harcourt Brace Jovanovich, 1982), p. 166.

White, David, "Antidog Days in Britain" (*Psychology Today*, August 1981), p. 12.

White, Margaret B., *Sharing Caring: The Art of Raising Kids in Two-Career Families* (Prentice-Hall, 1982).

Willis, Ellen, "The Politics of Dependency" (*Ms.*, June–August 1982), p. 182.